LETTERS ON DANCING

JEAN GEORGES NOVERRE
From the engraving by Sherwin

LETTERS

ON

DANCING

AND

BALLETS

BY

JEAN GEORGES NOVERRE

*Maître de Ballet to His Serene Highness the
Duke of Wurtemberg, and formerly of the
Principal Theatres of Paris, Lyon, Marseille,
London, etc.*

TRANSLATED BY

CYRIL W. BEAUMONT

*From the Revised and Enlarged Edition
published at St. Petersburg, 1803.*

ALTON
Dance Books
2004

First published in 1930 by C. W. Beaumont
This facsimile edition published in 2004 by Dance Books Ltd.,
The Old Bakery, 4 Lenten Street, Alton, Hampshire GU34 1HG
www.dancebooks.co.uk

Copyright © 2004 Imperial Society of Teachers of Dancing

ISBN 1 85273 100 1

Printed by Russell Press, Nottingham

This *English* Translation of JEAN GEORGES NOVERRE'S
Lettres sur la Danse et les Ballets is respectfully Inscribed

To MICHEL FOKINE

THE NOVERRE OF THE TWENTIETH CENTURY

As a slight token of admiration

from

THE TRANSLATOR

INTRODUCTION

JEAN GEORGES NOVERRE was born at Paris on April 27th, 1727. His father is said to have been of Swiss extraction and by profession an adjutant in the army of Charles XII. The son, intended for a military career, had been given an excellent education, but all his thoughts inclined towards the theatre, with the result that he was eventually placed as a pupil under the celebrated dancer Louis Dupré.

At the age of sixteen he appeared with Mlles. Puvigné and Lany at the Opéra Comique in a *pas de trois*, called *L'Acte des Fleurs*, in *L'Ambigu de la Folie, ou le Ballet des Dindons*, a parody of Rameau's *Indes Galantes*. Dissatisfied with his reception, he went to Potsdam at the invitation of Prince Henry of Prussia, but either the position or its emoluments did not please him and he returned to Paris. In 1747 he was appointed *maître de ballet* at the Opéra Comique where he produced a number of ballets. The year 1754 saw the performance at the Foire Saint Laurent of his *Fêtes Chinoises* and *La Fontaine de Jouvence*. The former was a notable production, the scenery being designed by François Boucher and the costumes by Boquet, who afterwards became Noverre's favourite designer.

Towards the end of that year, David Garrick, in search of some particular attraction to draw the public to Drury Lane, endeavoured to arrange for Noverre and his sister, together with a *corps de ballet* of his selection, to come to London. After a correspondence extending over many months, the contract was eventually signed on January 21st, 1755. According to its terms, Noverre was to receive for the season 350 guineas and a benefit, and his sister 100 guineas, Garrick to supply everything necessary for the production of the ballets ; the programme was to consist of *Les Fêtes Chinoises* and *La Fontaine de Jouvence*. Further, Noverre was authorised to engage the necessary dancers at 40 guineas apiece, and Boquet, in consideration of a fee of 150 guineas, was commissioned to design and supervise the making of the scenery and costumes, and plan the lighting of the ballets.

Unfortunately, the first performance on November 8th, 1755, of *The Chinese Festival*, to give the ballet its English title, coincided with a renewed feeling of bitterness between England and France, arising out of their struggle for colonial supremacy and the command of the sea. The countries were on the verge of the Seven Years' War, which officially broke out the following year. Garrick was fully aware of the difficulties attending his enterprise, but, being already committed to considerable expense, it was too late to withdraw. He inspired articles in the newspapers to the effect that Mr. Noverre and his sister were Swiss, and that of the 60 artistes engaged, two-thirds were English. Then he succeeded in inducing the king (George II) to honour the first performance with his presence.

The bill opened with *The Fair Quaker of Deal*, which passed off without incident, but the moment the curtain rose on the ballet a tremendous uproar ensued and the curtain had to be lowered. At each performance the attitude of the mob grew in violence and at the sixth they began to pull up the benches and tear down the scenery ; indeed, it was only with the greatest difficulty that they were prevented from firing the house. Garrick was obliged to announce from the stage that the ballet would not be repeated. The loss amounted to four thousand pounds.

On his return to Paris, Noverre endeavoured to obtain the post of *maître de ballet* to the Opéra. He was eager to place at the service of the country of his birth a completely new conception of ballet which the perfection of Garrick's acting had inspired in him. He enlisted the support of Madame de Pompadour to further his application which, however, was rejected.

In 1758, he obtained the post of *maître de ballet* to a large theatre at Lyon where he produced the comedy ballets : *Les Métamorphoses Chinoises, Les Réjouissances Flamandes, La Mariée de Village, La Fête du Vauxhall, Les Recrues Prussiennes, Le Bal Paré*; and the more serious ballets such as *La Mort d'Ajax, La Descente d'Orphée aux Enfers, Renaud et Armide, Les Caprices de Galatée, Le Toilette de Venus,*

Les Fêtes du Sérail, *L'Amour Corsaire* and *Le Jaloux sans Rival*.

Next he passed to Stuttgart to take up the position of *maître de ballet* to the Court of the Duke of Wurtemberg. Casanova, in the sixth volume of his *Mémoires*, sketches the almost unparalleled luxury of that prince's entertainments. At the period of 1760, France paid the Duke enormous subsidies in exchange for the loan of an army of 6,000 Wurtembergers. This money he expended prodigally on his pleasures. He had three theatres, one French and two Italian. The Prince did not do things by halves; he gave Noverre the services of Servandoni[1] as machinist and designer of scenery, Boquet[2] as designer of costumes, Jomelli as conductor, 20 principal dancers and 100 *danseurs* and *danseuses*.

Here Noverre produced the following ballets : *Les Amours d'Henri IV*, *La Jugement de Paris*, *Médée*, *Antoine et Cléopâtre*, *La Mort d'Hercule*, *Psyché*, *Diane et Endymion*, *Vénus et Adonis*, *Renaud et Armide*, *L'Enlèvement de Proserpine*, *Alexandre* and *Les Danaïdes*. Under his direction Stuttgart for eight years became the dancers' Mecca. Even the vainest of them, Gaetano Vestris, drawn there by curiosity, went away astonished and delighted by the infinite possibilities of the *ballet d'action*. He did all in his power to obtain for Noverre a hearing in Paris and, largely as a result of his representations, the *chorégraphe* visited that capital in 1765, when he produced at the Opéra his ballet *Médée*, which aroused the greatest interest.

In 1770, Noverre went to Vienna to direct the entertainments to be given on the occasion of the marriage of the Archduchess Caroline (Queen of Naples). He composed and produced several ballets for the Court Theatre : *Iphigénie en Tauride*, *Les Graces*, *Alceste*, *Enée et Didon*, *Adèle de Ponthieu*, *Les Horaces*, *Semiramis* and *La Mort d'Agamemnom*. He was appointed *maître de ballet* and Director of Court Entertainments, and also made *maître de danse* to the Empress Maria Theresa and the Imperial Family. In this way he taught dancing to her daughter Marie Antoinette.

[1] See footnote to p. 17.
[2] See footnote to p. 76.

From Vienna, Noverre went to Milan in 1774 to arrange a ballet on the occasion of another marriage, that of the Archduke Ferdinand of Austria with the Princess Beatrice of Modena. For this production, based on Ariosto's *Orlando Furioso*, he was made a Chevalier of the Order of Christ. While at Milan he produced many other ballets : *Apelles et Campaspe, La Rosière de Salency, La Foire du Caire, Ritiger et Wenda, Galéas—Duc de Milan, Euthymes et Eucharis, Belton et Eliza,* and *Hymenée et Cryséïs.* His engagements concluded, he went to the Court of Turin and afterwards to that of Naples.

In 1775, Noverre returned to Paris and, through the influence of his illustrious pupil, Marie Antoinette, now Queen of France, he was appointed in August, 1776, *maître de ballet* to the Académie Royale de Musique, in succession to Gaetano Vestris who had just tendered his resignation. This nomination was made without regard to the just claims of Maximilien Gardel and Dauberval, who, although disliking each other, joined against the common foe so that Noverre became the object of their hate and intrigue. But, in November, 1779, a compromise was reached by which Noverre promised to retire in their favour, on their being able to obtain for him a pension of 3,000 livres, together with that of an academician amounting to 500 livres.[1] On July 13th, 1780, the first pension was granted, but the second was withheld on the ground that the number of academicians was limited ; but he was informed that his claim would be granted when a vacancy occurred. A few days after the date cited he withdrew to St. Germain-en-Laye where he remained until the outbreak of the French Revolution.

It was not long before he felt the effects of the new order. First his pension was reduced to 375 francs. Then he became suspect as a person who had been on friendly terms with the " Austrian." Seeing the fine-meshed net closing about him, he fled to London, accompanied by many dancers and singers, including Vestris and Mlle. Guimard.

There, on January 29th, 1788, he produced his *L'Amour*

[1] The correspondence is given in Compardon (Emile), *L'Académie Royale de Musique.* 2 Vols. 1884. See Vol. II, pp. 202-216.

et Psyche with a company that included Vestris, Didelot and Coulon. On March 13th he staged *Euthyme et Eucharis* for Vestris's benefit, and on April 17th he gave *Adèle de Ponthieu*. The year following, on June 17th, the " King's " was burned to the ground. It was rebuilt in 1790 and reopened on March 26th, 1791, with Noverre as director, Vestris as *maître de ballet*, Haydn as composer, and Federici as conductor.

Noverre continued to produce ballets, including *Les Noces de Thétis* and *Iphigénie en Aulide*. His success was considerable and on one occasion the audience, carried away by enthusiasm, called for the author and crowned Noverre on the stage amid scenes reminiscent of the crowning of his admirer Voltaire at the Théâtre Français, during the sixth performance of *Irène* on March 30th, 1778. One of his last pieces was *Les Epoux du Tempe* given on January 26th, 1793.

For some time past Noverre had been in indifferent health, and the many buffets he both received and bestowed, in his efforts to reform the conception of ballet and elevate its status to that of the other arts, had sadly lowered his strength. In addition, all his savings had been dissipated by the Revolution and he was grief-stricken at the death by violence of so many of his royal and noble patrons. Reduced to comparative poverty, he returned to France and withdrew to St. Germain-en-Laye, where he died on October 18th, 1809.

*

* *

Noverre's *Letters*, considered as an exposition of the theories and laws governing ballet and dance representation, and as a contemporary history of dancing, have no equal in the whole of the literature devoted to the art, and no book has exerted so incalculable an influence for good on the manner of production of ballets and dances. Noverre was not only a most talented *chorégraphe*, but also a person possessed of an immense knowledge of his subject, and an unusual store of common sense and intelligence which he applied to the reform of every branch of his profession.

The book is contrived in the form of a series of letters,

in which he responds to all manner of questions relative to dancing, addressed to him by an imaginary correspondent. Noverre reformed stage costume, restored and developed the art of mime, emphasised the value of good music and decreed that all ballets must possess a good plot ; he insisted that a dance must be designed not as a mere *divertissement*, but as a means of expressing or assisting the development of the theme.

As an historical work, we can learn from its pages Noverre's opinion of the merits and defects of many of the great dancers of the first half of the eighteenth century, and glean the most valuable details regarding the production of, and costumes worn in, the ballets of the period.

Many dancers and students are familiar with the name of Noverre, but it is extraordinary how few have read his works, the value of whose sage counsels has, for the most part, depreciated little, despite the passing of some hundred and seventy years since their first publication.   It was not without reason that Garrick styled him : " The Shakespeare of the Dance," and that Voltaire concluded a letter to him with the words : " Vous êtes un Prométhée, il faut que vous formiez des hommes, et que vous les animiez."   Again, Carlo Blasis, in the Preface to his *Traité Elementaire, Théorique et Pratique de la Danse* (1820), in citing Noverre, remarks : " That celebrated artist's excellent letters on ballets have been written particularly for the composer and should never be out of his hands ; that work will teach artist-dancers the true dramatic laws and the simplest way to arouse interest in mimed action."

The *Lettres sur la Danse et les Ballets* was published at Stuttgart and at Lyon in 1760 ; at Vienna (dedicated to the Empress of Austria) in 1767 ; at London (dedicated to the Prince of Wales), in an English translation, in 1783 ; at Paris (dedicated to Monseigneur Amelot, Ministre au Département de Paris) in 1783 ; at Amsterdam in 1787 ; at Copenhagen in 1803 ; at St. Petersburg (dedicated to the Emperor of all the Russias) in 1803-4, this is a collected edition of Noverre's writings in four 4to volumes, with the general title : *Lettres sur la Danse, les Ballets et les Arts,* in addition to the Letters on Dancing, it contains the *scenarii* of a number of his ballets, his correspondence with Voltaire, and a number of letters on the Fine Arts generally ; at Paris (dedicated to the Empress of the French and Queen of Italy) in 1807, this is the collected works contained in two volumes, with the general title : *Lettres sur les Arts Imitateurs en Général et sur la Danse en Particulier.* The bi-centenary of Noverre's birth was marked by the publication at Paris, by Messrs. Duchartre and Buggenhoudt, of an *edition de luxe* of the Letters on Dancing, prefaced with a biography of the author by André Levinson.

The first and only English translation, already noted, is now rare and almost unobtainable ; it was made from the edition of 1783. I have worked from the revised and enlarged version of the Letters on Dancing contained in the beautiful St. Petersburg edition published by Schnoor, at the command and expense of the Emperor Alexander I, following a performance of Noverre's *Médée* reproduced by his pupil Le Picq ; this edition has an additional interest in that it contains a long Foreword by the author summing up the book's effect on dancing.

The present translation was published serially in *The Dancing Times* and is now reprinted by courtesy of the editor. I have revised the whole and added some notes for the use of dance students. In conclusion, I desire to record my very grateful thanks to my friend Mr. de V. Payen-Payne who, in addition to overlooking the proofs, afforded me many valuable suggestions.

CYRIL W. BEAUMONT

AUTHOR'S PREFACE

WHEN I decided to write on an art which is the continual object of my studies and reflections, I little foresaw the success and effect of my letters on dancing when they appeared in 1760. They were welcomed with interest by men of letters and persons of taste ; but, at the same time, they were received with spite and ill-humour by those for whom they were primarily designed. They aroused the indignation of nearly all the dancers of Europe, and especially those attached to the *Opéra* at Paris, which was, is, and will continue for a long time to be, the first and most magnificent of the temples of Terpsichore, but the votaries of which are the most pretentious and ill-humoured. Anathemas were hurled at me, I was treated as a reformer, and regarded as a man so much the more dangerous since I attacked the principles held in veneration owing to their antiquity.

When one has grown old in an art, whose laws one has followed and practised from childhood, it is difficult to go back to school again : idleness and self-esteem are both opposed to it ; it is as difficult to forget what one has acquired as to learn something new. The bitterness and disgust evoked by revolutions, of whatever kind, are always felt by persons of a certain age. The succeeding generations are always the ones to enjoy their useful and agreeable consequences.

To break hideous masks, to burn ridiculous perukes, to suppress clumsy paniers, to do away with still more inconvenient hip pads, to substitute taste for routine, to indicate a manner of dress more noble, more accurate and more picturesque, to demand action and expression in dancing, to demonstrate the immense distance which lies between mechanical technique and the genius which places dancing beside the imitative arts—all this was to expose myself to the ill-humour of those who respect and venerate the ancient laws and customs, however barbaric and ridiculous they might be. Again, when I received the praises and commendations of artists of all kinds, I was, on the other hand, the butt of the envy and satire of those for whom I wrote.

However, as in all arts, observations and principles drawn from nature always end by conquering. My opponents, although exclaiming that I was wrong, and rebutting my ideas, yet adopted them gradually. They came over more and more to my way of thinking, and unconsciously carried out my reforms, and soon I saw myself seconded by artists whose taste and imagination rising superior to their art, were far above sentiments of envy and jealousy.

M. Boquet, who had comprehended and adopted my views ; M. Dauberval, my pupil, who struggled continually against prejudice, custom and bad taste ; M. Vestris himself, who in his turn was struck by the truths which I had taught when he first saw them put into practice at Stuttgart; all these artists since become so celebrated, yielded to the evidence and ranged themselves under my banner. Soon, opera took a new line in regard to the costume, pomp and variety of its ballets, and the dancing in this style of entertainment, which, although still capable of further perfection, has become nevertheless the most brilliant in Europe, at last emerged from its long infancy ; it learned to speak the language of the passions which before it had not even lisped.

If one reflects on what opera was in 1760 and on what it is to-day,[1] it will be difficult not to recognise the effect produced by my letters. In fact they have been translated into Italian, German and English. The glory of my art, my age and my numerous brilliant successes, permit me to state that I have achieved a revolution in dancing, as striking and as lasting as that achieved by Gluck in the realm of music. The successes even by imitators to-day are the greatest testimony of the value of the principles which I have laid down in this work.

My letters were but the first stone of the monument which I desired to erect to that form of expressive dancing which the Greeks called pantomime.

[1] That is, in 1803.

Dancing, according to the accepted definition of the word, is the art of composing steps with grace, precision and facility to the time and bars given in the music, just as music itself is simply the art of combining sounds and modulations so that they afford pleasure to the ear. But the gifted musician does not confine himself to so limited a circle, and the distance he traverses beyond is much greater than the circle itself. He studies the character and accents of the passions and expresses them in his compositions. On the other hand, the *maître de ballet*, striking out beyond the customary limits of his art, seeks in these same passions their characteristic movements and gestures ; and binding with the same chain those steps, gestures and facial expressions to the sentiments he desires to express, he finds, in bringing together all these elements, the means of producing the most astonishing effects. It is well known to what degree the art of moving an audience by gesture was carried by the ancient mimes.

In this regard I shall even permit myself a reflection which comes naturally here, since it arises from the subject under discussion ; I submit and leave it to the judgment of those learned persons who have made a study of analysing our feelings.

At the performance of a play the feelings of each spectator are aroused in strength and intensity proportionate to his greater or lesser power of being affected. Now, from the least sensitive to the most sensitive spectator there is a multitude of shades of feeling, each of which is applicable to one of them, so that a quite natural conclusion must be reached. That is, that the author's dialogue must rise above or fall below the average responsiveness of the majority of the spectators. A cold and unemotional man will nearly always find the author's expressions exaggerated and even absurd, while the emotionable and excitable spectator will often find the action slow and tedious : whence I conclude that the playwright's thoughts seldom accord exactly with the responsiveness of the spectator ; unless the charm of the diction does not lay all the spectators under the same spell, an effect which I find difficult to conceive.

Pantomime, in my opinion, has not this drawback.

It is only necessary to indicate by the steps, gestures, movements and facial expression the sentiments of each person ; and it leaves to each spectator the task of imagining a dialogue which is ever true since it is always in accord with the emotions received.

This reflection has led me to examine with scrupulous attention all that takes place both at the performance of a pantomime ballet and at that of a play (supposing them to be of equal merit in their respective spheres). It has always seemed to me that in pantomime the effect is more general, more uniform and, if I may say so, more in consonance with the total feelings aroused by the performance.

I do not think that this thought is a purely metaphysical one. It has always appeared to me to express a truth easily comprehensible. There are, undoubtedly, a great many things which pantomime can only indicate, but in regard to the passions there is a degree of expression to which words cannot attain or rather there are passions for which no words exist. Then dancing allied with action triumphs. A step, a gesture, a movement, and an attitude express what no words can say ; the more violent the sentiments it is required to depict, the less able is one to find words to express them. Exclamations, which are the apex to which the language of passions can reach, become insufficient, and have to be replaced by gesture.

After reading these remarks one will realise the angle from which I looked at dancing from the moment I considered the subject, and how far in advance were my first ideas on that art in comparison with those then current. But, like the man who climbed to the summit of a mountain and saw the horizon stretch away before him, as I advanced in the career upon which I had just entered, I saw the path grow longer, as it were, at each step. I felt that dancing allied to action could be associated with all the imitative arts, and itself become one of them.

Since then, before selecting melodies to which I could adapt steps, before studying steps to make them into what was then known as a ballet, I sought subjects either in mythology, history or my own imagination which not only afforded opportunity for the introduction of dances and festivals, but which, in the course of the development of the theme, offered a graduated action and interest. My poem once conceived, I studied all the gestures, movements and expressions which could render the passions and sentiments arising from my theme. Only after concluding this labour did I summon music to my aid. Having explained to the composer the different details of the picture which I had just sketched out, I then asked him for music adapted to each situation and to each feeling. In place of writing steps to written airs, as couplets are set to known melodies, I composed, if I may so express myself, the dialogue of my ballet and then I had music written to fit each phrase and each thought.

Thus I explained to Gluck the characteristic air of the ballet of the savages in *Iphigénie in Tauride :* the steps, gestures, attitudes and expressions of the different characters which I outlined to him, gave to this celebrated composer the theme for that fine piece of music.

My ideas did not stop there. Pantomime being more of a performance for the eyes than for the ears, I thought that the arts which most please the sight should be brought in alliance with it. Painting, architecture, perspective and optics became the object of my studies. I composed no more ballets in which the laws relative to those different arts were not scrupulously observed, each time there arose an opportunity of employing them. It cannot but be realised that I must have made many reflections on each one separately, and on the general principles which unite them to one another. I set down on paper the thoughts born of my studies ; they were the object of a correspondence[1] in which I reviewed the different arts which are allied to dancing with action.

This correspondence gave me the opportunity to speak of the players who have enriched with their talents the different theatres in Europe. But this material entrusted to friends would certainly have been lost to the public and the arts if a circumstance, both worthy and unforeseen,

[1] A reference to Noverre's *Lettres sur les Arts Imitateurs* included in the Collected Works published at St. Petersburg, 1803, and for which the above Preface was written.

had not permitted me to-day to bring it together and make it public.

Like those intrepid navigators who brave storm and tempest to discover unknown lands from which they bring back objects to enrich science and art, commerce and industry, but whom insurmountable obstacles oppose in the midst of their travels, I confess that I have been forced to suspend mine. My sallies and efforts have been in vain, I have been unable to cross that barrier raised by impossibility and on which was written : *Thou shalt go no farther*.

I shall speak of these obstacles, and I shall prove that they cannot be vanquished. They are to the art of ballet with action what in former times the Pillars of Hercules were to navigators.

LIST OF ILLUSTRATIONS

The head-piece and tail-piece used throughout this book, and the cover, have been designed by RANDOLPH SCHWABE.

LETTERS ON DANCING

LETTER I

POETRY, painting and dancing, Sir, are, or should be, no other than a faithful likeness of beautiful nature. It is owing to their accuracy of representation that the works of men like Corneille and Racine, Raphael and Michelangelo, have been handed down to posterity, after having obtained (what is rare enough) the commendation of their own age. Why can we not add to the names of these great men those of the *maîtres de ballet*[1] who made themselves so celebrated in their day ? But they are scarcely known ; is it the fault of their art, or of themselves ?

A ballet is a picture, or rather a series of pictures connected one with the other by the plot which provides the theme of the ballet ; the stage is, as it were, the canvas on which the composer expresses his ideas ; the choice of the music, scenery and costumes are his colours ; the composer is the painter. If nature have endowed him with that passionate enthusiasm which is the soul of all imitative arts, will not immortality be assured him ? Why are the names of *maîtres de ballet* unknown to us ? It is because works of this kind endure only for a moment and are forgotten almost as soon as the impressions they had produced ; hence there remains not a vestige of the most sublime productions of a

---

[1] As a general rule, whenever Noverre uses the term *maître de ballet*, he employs it in its old sense of meaning the person who composes the dances in a *divertissement* or ballet. Nowadays, such a person is termed the *chorégraphe*, while the designation *maître de ballet* is applied to the individual responsible for the training of the dancers and the maintenance of their technique at the requisite standard of efficiency.

Bathyllus[1] and a Pylades.[1] Hardly a notion has been preserved of those pantomimes so celebrated in the age of Augustus.[2]

If these great composers, unable to transmit to posterity their fugitive pictures, had at least bequeathed us their ideas and the principles of their art ; if they had set forth the laws of the style of which they were the creators ; their names and writings would have traversed the immensity of the ages and they would not have sacrificed their labours and repose for a moment's glory. Those who have succeeded them would have had some principles to guide them, and the art of pantomime and gesture, formerly carried to a point which still astonishes the imagination, would not have perished.

Since the loss of that art, no one has sought to re-discover it, or, so to speak, to create it a second time. Appalled by the difficulties of that enterprise, my predecessors have abandoned it, without making a single attempt, and have allowed a divorce, which it would appear must be eternal, to exist between pure dancing and pantomime.

More venturesome than they, perhaps less gifted, I have dared to fathom the art of devising ballets with action ; to re-unite action with dancing ; to accord it some expression and purpose. I have dared to tread new paths, encouraged by the indulgence of the public which has supported me in crises capable of rebuffing one's self-esteem ; and my

---

[1] Bathyllus and Pylades were two celebrated mimes famous about 22 B.C. Bathyllus of Alexandria, the freedman and favourite of Mæcenas, together with Pylades of Cicilia and his pupil Hylas, brought to a fine degree of perfection, during the reign of Augustus, the imitative dance termed *Pantomimus*, which was one of the most popular public amusements at Rome until the fall of the Empire. Bathyllus excelled in the interpretation of comic scenes, while Pylades was unsurpassed in the representation of tragic themes. At first, the two actors gave performances in common, then, becoming jealous of each other's fame, they quarrelled and established rival theatres. Each founded a school and each had a numerous band of followers whose fierce partisanship led to many brawls and sometimes bloodshed

Some account of these actors will be found in Castil-Blaze. *La Danse et les Ballets*, 1832, Chapter I. For a description of their performances, consult Smith (W.). *A Dictionary of Greek and Roman Antiquities*. 2 Vols. 1891. Vol. 2, p. 334, *Pantomimus*.

[2] The first Emperor of the Roman Empire. Born Sept. 23rd, B.C. 63. Died Aug. 29th, A.D. 14.

successes appear to authorise me to satisfy your curiosity regarding an art which you cherish, and to which I have devoted my every moment.

From the reign of Augustus to our days, ballets have been only feeble sketches of what they may one day become. This art, born of genius and good taste, can become beautiful and varied to an infinite degree. History, legend, painting, all the arts may unite to withdraw their sister art from the obscurity in which she is shrouded ; and it astonishes one that *maîtres de ballet* have disdained such powerful assistance.

The programmes of the ballets which have been given, during the past century or so, in the different courts of Europe, incline one to believe that this art (which was still of no account), far from having progressed, is more and more declining. These kinds of traditions, it is true, are always strongly suspect. It is with ballets as with entertainments in general ; nothing so grandiose and so alluring on paper, and often nothing so dull and ill-arranged in performance.

I think, Sir, that this art has remained in its infancy only because its effects have been limited, like those of fireworks designed simply to gratify the eyes ; although this art shares with the best plays the advantage of inspiring, moving and captivating the spectator by the charm of its interest and illusion. No one has suspected its power of speaking to the heart.

If our ballets be feeble, monotonous and dull, if they be devoid of ideas, meaning, expression and character, it is less, I repeat, the fault of the art than that of the artist : does he ignore that dancing united to pantomime is an imitative art ? I shall be tempted to believe it, because the majority of composers restrict themselves to making a servile copy of a certain number of steps and figures to which the public has been treated for centuries past ; in such wise that the ballets from *Phaéton*,[1] or from another opera, revived by a modern composer, differ so little from those of the

[1] A lyrical tragedy in five acts and a prologue, with libretto by Quinault and music by Lully. It was first played before the Court on Jan. 6th, 1663. The first public performance was given at the Académie Royale de Musique, on April 27th, of the same year. It had an immense success due to its many charming airs and the wealth of the mechanical effects introduced. Its theme was the return of the Golden Age, and it was intended as a panegyric in honour of Louis XIV.

past that one would imagine they were always the same.

In fact, it is rare, not to say impossible, to find genius in the plans, elegance in the forms, lightness in the groups, precision and neatness in the tracks which lead to the different figures ; the art of disguising old things and giving them an air of novelty is scarcely known.

Maîtres de ballet should consult the pictures of great painters. This examination would undoubtedly bring them in touch with nature ; then they should avoid, as often as possible, that symmetry in the figures which, repeating the same thing, offers two similar pictures on the same canvas. That is not to say that I condemn in general all symmetrical figures or to think that I claim to abolish the practice entirely, for that would be to misinterpret my views.

The abuse of the best things is always detrimental ; I only disapprove of the too frequent and too repeated use of these kinds of figures, a practice which my colleagues will feel to be vicious when they essay to copy nature faithfully and to depict on the stage different passions with the shades and colours which appertain to each in particular.

Symmetrical figures from right to left are, in my opinion, only supportable in the *corps d'entrées*,[1] which have no means of expression, and which, conveying nothing, are employed simply to give the *premiers danseurs* time to take breath ; they can have a place in a *ballet général* which concludes a festival ; further, they can be tolerated in *pas d'execution, pas de quatre, pas de six*, etc., although, to my mind, it would be ridiculous, in these fragments, to sacrifice expression and feeling to bodily skill and agility of the legs ; but symmetry should give place to nature in *scènes d'action*. One example, however slight it may be, will make my meaning clear and suffice to support my contention.

A band of nymphs, at the unexpected sight of a troupe of young fauns, takes flight hurriedly in fear ; the fauns,

[1] An *entrée* is a *divertissement* executed by a number of dancers.

Compan, in his *Dictionnaire de Danse* (1787) gives the following definition : " The usual division for all kinds of ballets is five acts. Each act consists of three, six, nine, and sometimes twelve *entrées*. The term *entrée* is given to one or more bands of dancers who, by means of their steps, gestures and attitudes, express that portion of the whole theme which has been assigned to them."

on their side, pursue the nymphs with eagerness, which generally suggests delight : presently, they stop to examine the impression they have made on the nymphs ; at the same time the latter suspend their course ; they regard the fauns with fear, seek to discover their designs, and to attain by flight a refuge which would secure them against the danger which threatens ; the two troupes approach ; the nymphs resist, defend themselves and escape with a skill equal to their agility, etc.

That is what I term a *scène d'action*, where the dance should speak with fire and energy ; where symmetrical and formal figures cannot be employed without transgressing truth and shocking probability, without enfeebling the action and chilling the interest. There, I say, is a scene which should offer a ravishing disorder, and where the composer's art should not appear except to embellish nature.

A *maître de ballet*, devoid of intelligence and good taste, will treat this portion of the dance mechanically, and deprive it of its effect, because he will not feel the spirit of it. He will place the nymphs and the fauns on several parallel lines, he will scrupulously exact that all the nymphs be posed in uniform attitudes, and that the fauns have their arms raised at the same height ; he will take great care in his arrangement not to place five nymphs to the right and seven to the left, for this would transgress the traditions of the *Opéra*, but he will make a cold and formal performance of a *scène d'action* which should be full of fire.

Some ill-disposed critics, who do not understand enough of the art to judge of its different effects, will say that this scene should offer two pictures only ; that the desire of the fauns should express one, and the fear of the nymphs depict the other. But how many different gradations are there to contrive in that fear and that desire ; what oppositions, what variations of light and shade to observe ; so that from these two sentiments there result a multitude of pictures, each more animated than the other !

All men having the same passions, differ only in proportion to their sensibilities ; they affect with more or less force all men, and manifest themselves outwardly with more or less vehemence and impetuosity. This principle stated, which nature demonstrates every day, one should vary the attitudes, diffuse the shades of expression, and thenceforth the pantomimic action of each person would cease to be monotonous.

It would result in being both a faithful imitator and an excellent painter, to put variety in the expression of the heads, to give an air of ferocity to some of the fauns, to others less passion ; to these a more tender air, and, lastly, to the others a voluptuous character which would calm or share the fear of the nymphs. The sketch of this picture determines naturally the composition of the other : I see then the nymphs who hesitate between pleasure and fear, I perceive others who, by their contrasting attitudes, depict to me the different emotions with which their being is agitated ; the latter are prouder than their companions, the former mingle fear with a sense of curiosity which renders the picture more seductive ; this variety is the more attractive in its likeness to nature. You must agree with me, Sir, that symmetry should always be banished from dances with action.

I will ask those who usually are prejudiced, if they will find symmetry in a flock of stray sheep which wish to escape from the murdering fangs of wolves, or in a band of peasants who abandon their fields and hamlets to avoid the fury of the enemy who pursues them ? No, without a doubt; but true art consists in concealing art. I do not counsel disorder and confusion at all, on the contrary I desire that regularity be found even in irregularity ; I ask for ingenious groups, strong but always natural situations, a manner of composition which conceals the composer's labours from the eyes of the spectator.

As to figures, they only deserve to please when they are presented in quick succession and designed with both taste and elegance.

I am, &c.

LETTER II

I CANNOT refrain, Sir, from expressing my disapproval of those *maîtres de ballet* who have the ridiculous obstinacy to insist that the members of the *corps de ballet* shall take them as a model and regulate their movements, gestures and attitudes accordingly. May not such a singular claim prevent the development of the executants' natural graces and stifle their innate powers of expression ?

This principle appears to me the more dangerous in that it is rare to meet with *maîtres de ballet* capable of real feeling ; so few of them are excellent actors competent to depict in gesture the thoughts they wish to express. It is so difficult, I say, to meet with a modern Bathyllus or Pylades, that I cannot avoid condemning all those who, from self-conceit, have the pretension to imitate them. If their powers of emotion be weak, their powers of expression will be likewise ; their gestures will be feeble, their features characterless, and their attitudes devoid of passion. Surely, to induce the *figurants* to copy so mediocre a model is to lead them astray ? Is not a production marred when it is awkwardly executed ? Moreover, is it possible to lay down fixed rules for pantomimic action ? Are not gestures the offspring of feeling and the faithful interpreters of every mood ?

In these circumstances, a careful *maître de ballet* should act like the majority of poets who, having neither the talent nor the natural gifts necessary to declamation, have their works recited and rely entirely on the intelligence of the actors for their interpretation. They are present, you will say, at the rehearsals. I agree, but less to lay down precepts than to offer advice. " This scene appears to me feeble ; in another, your delivery is weak ; this incident is not acted with sufficient fire, and the picture which results from that situation leaves something to be desired " : that is how the poet speaks. The *maître de ballet*, for his part, must continually rehearse a mimed scene until the performers have arrived at that moment of expression innate in mankind, a precious moment which is revealed with both strength and truth when it is the outcome of feeling.

A well-composed ballet is a living picture of the passions, manners, customs, ceremonies and customs of all nations of the globe, consequently, it must be expressive in all its details and speak to the soul through the eyes ; if it be devoid of expression, of striking pictures, of strong situations, it becomes a cold and dreary spectacle. This form of art will not admit of mediocrity ; like the art of painting, it exacts a perfection the more difficult to acquire in that it is dependent on the faithful imitation of nature ; and it is by no means easy, if not almost impossible, to seize on that kind of seductive truth which, masking illusion from the spectator, transports him in a moment to the spot where the action has taken place and fills him with the same thoughts that he would experience were he to witness in reality the incident which art has presented to him in counterfeit. What accuracy is required to avoid passing above, or falling below, the model it is desired to copy ! To over-refine a model is as dangerous as to disfigure it : these two faults are equally opposed to truth ; the one transcends nature, the other degrades it.

Ballets, being representations, should unite the various parts of the drama. Themes expressed in dancing are, for the most part, devoid of sense, and offer a confused medley of scenes as ill-connected as they are ill-ordered ; however, in general, it is imperative to submit to certain principles. The subject of every ballet must have its introduction, plot and climax. The success of this type of entertainment depends partly on the careful choice of subjects and their arrangement.

The art of pantomime is undoubtedly much more limited to-day than it was in the reign of Augustus ; there are so many things that cannot be rendered intelligibly by gesture alone. If the composer have not the skill to prune his theme of all that appears to him cold and dull, his ballet will never make a sensation. If M. Servandoni's[1] production failed to succeed, it was not due to any lack of gesture, for his actors' arms were never at rest ; nevertheless, his pantomimic exhibitions were as cold as ice, and an hour and a half of movements and gestures did not afford a single picture worthy of a painter's attention.

Diana and Acteon, Diana and Endymion, Apollo and Daphne, Tito and Aurora, Acis and Galatea, as well as all other themes of this nature, cannot provide the plot for a *ballet d'action* without the inspiration of truly poetic genius. Telemachus, in the Isle of Calypso, offers a wider field and would provide the theme for a very fine ballet,[2] always presuming the composer had the skill to omit everything of no value to a painter, to introduce Mentor at the right moment, and to remove him the instant his presence became superfluous.

If the licence that is taken daily in theatrical productions cannot be stretched so far as to make Mentor dance in the ballet of Telemachus, then it is a more than sufficient reason that the composer should not employ this character save with the greatest caution. If he do not dance he is foreign to the ballet, besides, his powers of expression, being deprived of the graces which dancing affords to gestures and attitudes, would make him appear less animated, less passionate, and consequently of less interest. A genius may break ordinary rules and advance by new paths when they lead to the perfection of his art.

[1] Giovanni Geremia Servandoni, a celebrated Italian architect and painter; born at Florence, May 22nd, 1695, died at Paris, Jan. 29th, 1766. He studied painting at Florence, later at Rome. Panini was his master for painting, Rossi his teacher in architecture. When travelling in Portugal he was asked to design a series of stage decorations for the theatre at Lisbon, which he executed with considerable success. He went to Paris in 1724 and began to plan scenery for the Académie Royale de Musique. In 1732, he was made architect to the king. He also designed scenery for the theatres at Dresden and Stuttgart. He was particularly skilled in the planning of decorations for public fêtes. According to contemporaries, he was possessed of great ability and gifted with considerable imagination. Prodigal in money matters he left little estate, although he worked hard all his life ; but his ambition was concentrated upon the acquisition of fame rather than wealth.

[2] In this connection it is of interest to note that Pierre Gabriel Gardel wrote a *ballet-héroïque* in three acts entitled *Télémaque dans l'Isle de Calypso* (pub. 1790) and d'Auberval (*i.e.*, Jean Bercher) wrote a *ballet pantomime* in three acts with the same title (pub. 1791).

Mentor, in a ballet, can and ought to dance. This will offend against neither truth nor probability, provided that the composer has the skill to devise for him a manner of dancing and expression consonant with his character, age and employment. I believe, Sir, that I would hazard the adventure, and that I should avoid the greater of two evils, that sense of tedium which should never be experienced by the spectator.

It is a capital fault to associate opposite styles and to mix them without distinction ; the serious with the comic, the noble with the trivial, the elegant with the burlesque. These gross faults, sufficiently common to many *maîtres de ballet*, reveal poverty of imagination ; they proclaim the composer's ignorance and bad taste. The character and style of a ballet must never be disfigured by episodes opposed in style and character, and the transformations and scenic changes commonly made use of by rope-dancers in English pantomimes[1] cannot be employed in exalted themes ; again, it is a mistake to repeat the same incident two or three times in succession, this repetition of scenes chills the action and impoverishes the theme.

Undoubtedly, one of the essential points in a ballet is variety ; the incidents and pictures which result from it should succeed each other with rapidity ; if the action do not move quickly, if the scenes drag, if enthusiasm be not communicated everywhere equally ; indeed, if the ballet do not constantly increase in interest and attraction in proportion to the development of the theme ; the plan is ill-conceived, ill-ordered ; it sins against the laws of the theatre, and the representation has no other effect on the spectator than that of the boredom induced by it.

I have seen—would you credit it, Sir ?—four similar scenes in the same ballet ; I have seen furniture provide the introduction, plot and climax of a grand ballet ; lastly, I have seen burlesque episodes associated with the most

---

[1] Probably a reference to the pantomimes first devised by John Rich in 1717, and generally presented at the Lincoln's Inn Fields Theatre, which took the town by storm. The great feature of these entertainments was the introduction of all kinds of wonderful scenic effects and transformations ; such as trees changed into houses, shops into serpents and ostriches, and men and women into wheel-barrows and stools.

exalted and passionate themes—the action passed in one of the most venerated spots in all Asia—do not such stupidities shock good taste ? Personally, I should have been little astonished if I had not known the composer's merit, which has almost convinced me that there is more indulgence in the capital than anywhere else.

Every complicated and long-drawn-out ballet which does not explain to me, simply and clearly, the action which it represents, the plot of which I cannot follow without constant reference to the programme—every ballet of which I do not understand the plan, which does not afford me an introduction, plot and climax—will be no more, in my opinion, than a simple entertainment based on dancing, more or less well executed. It will move me but little, since it will be expressionless and devoid of action and interest.

But the dancing of our time is beautiful, it will be said, able to captivate and please, even when it does not possess the feeling and wit with which you wish it to be embellished. I will admit that the mechanical execution of that art has been brought to a degree of perfection which leaves nothing to be desired ; I will even add that it often has grace and nobility ; but these represent only a portion of the qualities which it should possess.

Steps, the ease and brilliancy of their combination, equilibrium, stability, speed, lightness, precision, the opposition of the arms with the legs—these form what I term the mechanism of the dance. When all these movements are not directed by genius, and when feeling and expression do not contribute their powers sufficiently to affect and interest me, I admire the skill of the human machine, I render justice to its strength and ease of movement, but it leaves me unmoved ; it does not affect me or cause me any more sensation than this arrangement of the following words : *Fait. . .pas. . .le. . .la. . .honte. . .non. . .crime. . .et. . .l'échafaud.* But when these words are ordered by a poet they compose this beautiful line spoken by the Comte d'Essex :—

Le crime fait la honte, et non pas l'échafaud.[1]

[1] The crime causes the shame and not the scaffold. A celebrated passage from Act 4, Scene 3 of the *Comte d'Essex* (1678) by the playwright Thomas Corneille (1625–1709). The phrase is imitated from Tertullian—*martyrem fecit causa, non poena.*

It may be concluded from this comparison that dancing is possessed of all the advantages of a beautiful language, yet it is not sufficient to know the alphabet alone.   But when a man of genius arranges the letters to form words and connects the words to form sentences, it will cease to be dumb ; it will speak with both strength and energy ; and then ballets will share with the best plays the merit of affecting and moving, and of making tears flow, and, in their less serious styles, of being able to amuse, captivate and please.   And dancing, embellished with feeling and guided by talent, will at last receive that praise and applause which all Europe accords to poetry and painting, and the glorious rewards with which they are honoured.

I am, &c.

LETTER III

IF strong passions be proper to tragedy, they are no less compulsory to the art of pantomime. Our art is subject, in some manner, to the laws of perspective; minor details are absorbed in the distance. So, in pictures presented through the medium of dancing, there must be striking features, strong situations, well-defined character, bold masses with contrasts of light and shade both arresting and artistically contrived.

It is somewhat strange that, hitherto, it has seemed to be ignored that the style most suitable for expression in terms of dancing is the tragic; it offers fine pictures, noble incidents and excellent theatrical effects; moreover, the imitation of them is easier and the pantomimic action more expressive, more natural and more intelligible.

A skilful *maître de ballet* should be able to divine at a glance the general effect of the performance in its entirety, and never sacrifice the whole to the part.

Without forgetting the principal players in the piece, he should give consideration to the performers as a body; if he concentrate his attention on the *premières danseuses* and *premiers danseurs*, the action becomes tedious, the progress of the scenes drawn out, and the execution has no power of attraction.

In the tragedy of *Mérope*,[1] the principal characters are Mérope, Polyphonte, Egisthe and Narbas; but although the other actors are not charged with such important parts, they contribute none the less to the general action and dramatic development, which would be broken and suspended if one of these characters were missing from a performance of that piece.

[1] A play by Voltaire.

Not a single, unnecessary personage should appear to the spectator, consequently the stage should be denuded of everything likely to retard the action and only the exact number of persons introduced whose presence is required for the performance of the drama.

A *ballet d'action* should be constructed similarly ; it should be divided into scenes and acts, and each scene should possess, like the act, a beginning, central portion and conclusion ; that is to say, its introduction, plot and climax.

I have already observed that the principal persons in a ballet should not efface the minor actors.   I even think that it is less difficult to allot striking parts to Hercules and Omphale, to Ariadne and Bacchus, to Ajax and Ulysses, etc., than to the four-and-twenty persons in their train. If they express nothing on the stage, they are superfluous and should be removed ; if they mean something, their bearing should always be consonant with that of the principal actors.

The difficulty does not consist in assigning a dominant and distinctive part to Ajax and Ulysses, since this arises naturally from their position in the play.   The difficulty lies in finding a sufficient reason for the introduction of the *figurants*, in providing them with more or less important parts to connect them with the doings of the two heroes, in adroitly introducing women into this ballet, in making some of them participate in Ajax's predicament and the majority favour Ulysses. The triumph of the latter and the death of his rival afford the artist a series of the most seductive images, each more picturesque than the other, and in which the contrasts of light and shade should produce the most lively sensations.

After my explanations, it is easy to perceive that ballet-pantomime should always be concerned with action, and that the *figurants* should not replace the actor who has left the stage, except to fill it in their turn, not by a number of symmetrical figures and formal steps, but by a lively and animated expression which keeps the spectator always attentive to the theme which the preceding actors have explained.

Yet, whether owing to an unfortunate custom, or from ignorance, there are few rational ballets ; dancing is introduced for the mere sake of dancing ; and it would seem that everything consisted in the movement of the legs, in high jumps, and that the idea of what, according to people of taste, a ballet should be, is completely fulfilled when it consists of performers who do nothing, who mingle and jostle with one another, who offer only dull and confused pictures designed without taste, grouped ungracefully and devoid of all harmony and that expression, the offspring of the soul, which alone can adorn the ballet by giving it life.

Nevertheless, it must be conceded that trifling beauties and sparks of genius are sometimes to be found in these kinds of compositions. But very few of them can exhibit a perfect whole. The picture will be deficient either in composition or in colour, or, if it be correctly designed, it will lack, perhaps, taste, grace and imagination.

Do not include from what I have remarked above concerning *figurants* and *figurantes* that they should play parts equal in importance to those of the *premiers sujets*, but, since the action in a ballet begins to drag if it be not general, I maintain that the former should take part in it with art and skill, because it is important that the players charged with principal parts should retain their value and superiority over those that surround them. The art of the composer then is to bring together all his ideas to one common point so that the workings of his mind and genius are combined. By this means the characters will appear in a pleasing light and be neither sacrificed to, nor effaced by, those things which are only employed to give them strength and relief.

A *maître de ballet* should endeavour to accord to each of his dancers a different action, expression and character. They should all contribute to the same end, but by different means, and, always acting in unanimous concert, should depict by the fidelity of their gestures and imitation, the theme which the composer has been at pains to invent for them. If a ballet be dominated by uniformity, if that diversity of expression, form, attitude and character found in nature be absent, if those delicate but truthful shades which depict the same passions more or less forcibly, and in more or less bright colours, be not managed with skill and distributed with taste and intelligence, then the picture is, at best, but a poor copy of an excellent original, and, since it bears no relation to truth, has neither the power nor the right to move or affect the spectator.

What shocked me in the ballet *Diane et Endymion*, which I saw performed at Paris some years ago, was less the mechanical execution than the ill-arranged plan. What an idea to choose for movement, the very moment when Diana is about to afford Endymion proofs of her affection! Can the composer be excused for associating peasants with that goddess, to make them eye-witnesses of her frailty and passion? Is it possible to err more grossly against probability? According to the fable, Diana only visited Endymion when night held her court, the hour when mortals are fast in sleep; does not this exclude all attendants? The god of love alone might have been present; but peasants, nymphs, Diana hunting: what licence! what utter nonsense! or, better, what ignorance! It is easy to perceive that the author had only an imperfect conception of the fable of Endymion, which he has confused with that of Acteon, who surprised Diana bathing with her nymphs. The plot of the ballet was no less strange; the nymphs, represented as paragons of chastity, wished to slay both the god of love and the shepherd, but Diana, less virtuous than her followers, and carried away by the strength of her passions, opposed their fury and hastened to ward off their blows. The god of love, to punish this excess of virtue, made the nymphs amorous. They passed with rapidity from hate to tenderness, and the god caused them to fall into the arms of the peasants. You observe, Sir, that this theme is opposed to all rule, and that the ordering of it is as deficient in imagination as it is false. In my opinion, the composer sacrificed everything to effect, seduced by the scene of the arrows drawn ready to pierce the god of love, but this incident was misplaced. Besides, the picture was untrue; the nymphs were given the character of the Bacchantes who tore Orpheus to pieces. Diana was less a lover than a fury. Endymion, barely grateful and little moved by the action on his behalf, appeared not so much tender as indifferent: the god of love was simply a timid child, frightened by the noise, who fled through fear; such were the deficient characters which weakened the picture, destroyed its effect and proved the ineptitude of the composer.

Maîtres de ballet who wish to possess a just notion of their art should examine with attention the battles of Alexander depicted by Le Brun,[1] or those of Louis XIV painted by Van der Meulen ;[2] they will remark that these two heroes, who are the principal subjects of each painting, are not the sole object of interest to the spectator. That prodigious number of combatants, of vanquished and victors, agreeably divide the spectator's admiration and contribute mutually to the perfection and beauty of these masterpieces ; each head has its own expression and particular character, each attitude has strength and energy, the groupings of the wounded and fallen are both picturesque and ingenious ; everything has meaning and arouses interest because everything contributes to the general effect. Then, afterwards, if a veil be thrown over those portions of the pictures which represent sieges, battles, trophies and victories so that the two heroes alone are seen, the interest will be enfeebled : there will only remain the portraits of two great princes.

Pictures demand action, details, a certain number of persons whose character, attitudes and gestures should be at once true, natural and expressive. If the enlightened onlooker do not, at the first glance, unravel the painter's intention, if the historical episode which he has chosen do not quickly recur to the spectator's memory, the arrangement is defective, the situation ill-chosen, and the composition obscure and without taste.

The difference between the picture and the portrait should be similarly accepted in dancing. Ballets, as I understand them and as they ought to be, are alone worthy of this appellation ; those, on the contrary, which are monotonous and devoid of expression, which exhibit only indifferent and imperfect copies of nature, can only be termed meretricious and lifeless displays.

[1] Charles Le Brun (1619-1690), a celebrated French artist. In 1648 he founded, with Colbert, The Academy of Painting and Sculpture. His pompous style of painting found high favour with Louis XIV, who commissioned him to execute a series of pictures based on episodes in the life of Alexander the Great. Le Brun's pictures, although deficient in drawing and colour, are remarkable for their vigour of conception.

[2] Antony Francis Van der Meulen (1634-1690), a Flemish painter called to Paris about 1666 by Colbert, at the request of Le Brun, to fill the post of battle painter to Louis XIV.

A ballet is either the likeness of a finished painting or the original. You will tell me, perhaps, that a painter needs only one moment and in a single stroke of his brush he will give life to his canvas, but a ballet is a sequence of circumstances productive of a multitude of incidents. In that we are agreed, and, in order that my comparison may be the more effective, I will draw a parallel between a *ballet d' action* and the gallery of the Luxembourg painted by Rubens. Each picture presents a scene which leads on naturally to another and thence to the climax, and the eye, without trouble or hindrance, deciphers the history of a prince whose memory, through love and gratitude, has been deeply engraved on the heart of every Frenchman.

I hold the opinion, Sir, that it is no less difficult for a painter and a *maître de ballet* to devise a poem or a drama in painting or dancing, than it is for a poet to compose one ; for, if genius be wanting, nothing can be achieved ; one cannot paint with the legs since, if steps be not guided by the dancers' brains, they will always go astray, and their execution will be mechanical—and what is the art of dancing when it is limited to the execution of certain steps with a monotonous regularity ?

I am, &c.

LETTER IV

DANCING and ballets, Sir, have become the vogue of the day; they are received with a kind of passion and never was an art more encouraged by applause than our own. The French stage, the richest in Europe in dramas of all kinds and the most prolific in eminent performers, has been forced in some degree, in order to gratify the public taste and to be in the fashion, to include dancing in its programmes.

The lively and pronounced taste for ballets is general; every sovereign employs them to adorn his stage spectacles, not so much to copy our customs, as to minister to the eager interest which this art excites. The most insignificant touring company trails after it a swarm of dancers of both sexes, indeed, charlatans and vendors of quack medicines have more confidence in the merit of their ballets than in their nostrums; it is with *entrechats* that they attract the staring eyes of the crowd, and the sales of their remedies rise and fall accordingly as their entertainments are more or less numerous.

The indulgence with which the public applauds such trifles should, in my opinion, urge the artist to seek perfection. Praise should encourage and not dazzle us with the idea that the highest achievement has been attained and that there remains nothing more to accomplish. The false confidence resident in the majority of *maîtres de ballet*, and the little trouble they take to attain further improvement, inclines me to suspect that they imagine they have nothing more to learn.

The public, for its part, takes delight in deluding itself that the taste and talents of its time are far superior to those of preceding epochs; hence the florid steps and grimaces of our dancers are received with the most enthusiastic applause. I am not speaking of that section of the public which is its life and soul, of those intelligent men who, incapable of being swayed by popular prejudice, deplore the bad taste of their contemporaries, who listen without talking, who regard everything with attention, who consider carefully before they judge, and only applaud those passages which move, affect and transport them. That applause lavished at a whim and without discernment, often proves the ruin of young men training for a stage career. I know that applause is the food of the arts, but it ceases to be wholesome if administered indiscriminately ; and the nutrition is so rich that, far from strengthening the constitution, it disturbs and enfeebles it. Stage beginners are similar to those children totally spoiled by the blind affection of their parents. Faults and imperfections are perceived as the illusion wears off and the attraction of novelty diminishes.

Painting and dancing have this advantage over the other arts, that they are of every country, of all nations ; that their language is universally understood, and that they achieve the same impression everywhere.

If our art, imperfect as it is, seduce and captivate the spectator : if dancing stripped of the charm of expression sometimes occasion us trouble and emotion, and throw our thoughts into a pleasing disorder ; what power and domination might it not achieve over us if its movements were directed by brains and its pictures painted with feeling ? There is no doubt that ballets will rival painting in attraction when the executants display less of the automaton and the composers are better trained.

A fine picture is but the image of nature ; a finished ballet is nature herself, embellished with every ornament of the art. If a painted canvas convey to me a sense of illusion, if I am carried away by the skill of the delineator, if I am moved by the sight of a picture, if my captivated thoughts are affected in a lively manner by this enchantment, if the colours and brush of the skilful artist react on my senses so as to reveal to me nature, to endow her with speech so that I fancy I hear and answer her, how shall my feelings be wrought upon, what shall I become, and what will be my sensations, at the sight of a representation still more veracious and rendered by the histrionic abilities of my fellow-creatures ? What dominion will not living and varied pictures possess over my imagination ? Nothing interests man so much as humanity itself. Yes, Sir, it is shameful that dancing should renounce the empire it might assert over the mind and only endeavour to please the sight. A beautiful ballet is, up to the present, a thing seen only in the imagination ; like the Phœnix it is never found.

It is a vain hope to re-model the dance, so long as we continue to be slaves to the old methods and ancient traditions of the *Opéra*. At our theatres we see only feeble copies of the copies that have preceded them ; let us not practise steps only, let us study the passions. In training ourselves to feel them, the difficulty of expressing them will vanish, then the features will receive their impressions from the sentiments within, they will give force to exterior movements and paint in lines of fire the disorder of the senses and the tumult which reigns in the breast.

Dancing needs only a fine model, a man of genius, and ballets will change their character. Let this restorer of the true dance appear, this reformer of bad taste and of the vicious customs that have impoverished the art ; but he must appear in the capital. If he would persuade, let him open the eyes of our young dancers and say to them :—
" Children of Terpsichore, renounce *cabrioles*, *entrechats* and over-complicated steps ; abandon grimaces to study sentiments, artless graces and expression ; study how to make your gestures noble, never forget that it is the life-blood of dancing ; put judgment and sense into your *pas de deux ;* let will-power order their course and good taste preside over all situations ; away with those lifeless masks but feeble copies of nature ; they hide your features, they stifle, so to speak, your emotions and thus deprive you of your most important means of expression ; take off those enormous wigs and those gigantic head-dresses which destroy the true proportions of the head with the body ; discard the use of those stiff and cumbersome hoops which detract from the beauties of execution, which disfigure the elegance of your attitudes and mar the beauties of contour which the bust should exhibit in its different positions.

" Renounce that slavish routine which keeps your art in its infancy ; examine everything relative to the develop-

ment of your talents ; be original ; form a style for yourselves
based on your private studies ; if you must copy, imitate
nature, it is a noble model and never misleads those who
follow it.

" As for you young men who aspire to be *maîtres de ballet*
and think that to achieve success it is sufficient to have
danced a couple of years under a man of talent, you must
begin by acquiring some of this quality yourselves.   Devoid
of enthusiasm, wit, imagination, taste and knowledge, would
you dare set up as painters ?   You wish for an historical
theme and know nothing of history !   You fly to poets and
are unacquainted with their works !   Apply yourselves to
the study of them so that your ballets will be complete
poems.   Learn the difficult art of selection.   Never undertake great enterprises without first making a careful plan ;
commit your thoughts to paper ; read them a hundred times
over ; divide your drama into scenes ; let each one be
interesting and lead in proper sequence, without hindrance
or superfluities, to a well-planned climax ; carefully eschew
all tedious incidents, they hold up the action and spoil its
effect.   Remember that *tableaux* and groups provide the
most delightful moments in a ballet.

" Make your *corps de ballet* dance, but, when it does so,
let each member of it express an emotion or contribute to
form a picture ; let them mime while dancing so that the
sentiments with which they are imbued may cause their
appearance to be changed at every moment.   If their gestures
and features be constantly in harmony with their feelings,
they will be expressive accordingly and give life to the
representation.   Never go to a rehearsal with a head stuffed
with new figures and devoid of sense.   Acquire all the knowledge you can of the matter you have in hand.   Your
imagination, filled with the picture you wish to represent,
will provide you with the proper figures, steps and gestures.
Then your compositions will glow with fire and strength,
they cannot but be true to nature if you are full of your
subject.   Bring love as well as enthusiasm to your art.
To be successful in theatrical representations, the heart must
be touched, the soul moved and the imagination inflamed.

" Are you, on the contrary, lukewarm ?   Does your blood
circulate slowly through your veins ?   Have you a heart

of ice ? Have you a soul incapable of sensation ? Then renounce the stage, abandon an art for which you are unfitted. Adopt a profession or trade where imagination is of no account, with which genius has nothing to do and wherein you have need of arms and hands only."

If, Sir, the principles pronounced were followed, the stage would be disencumbered of an inestimable quantity of indifferent dancers and of bad *maîtres de ballet*, while the blacksmith's trade and others would be supplied with a number of workers much more usefully employed in administering to the wants of society, than they can ever be of service in contributing to its amusements and entertainments.

I am, &c.

LETTER V

TO convince you, Sir, of the difficulty of excelling in our art, I wish to outline the knowledge we should possess ; knowledge which, indispensable as it is, does not, however, provide the distinguishing mark of a *maître de ballet*, because one may possess it and still be incapable of composing the least *tableau*, of creating the most insignificant group and of imagining the most unimportant situation.

To judge from the prodigious quantity of *maîtres de ballet* of this type who can be found scattered over Europe, one would be tempted to believe that this art is as easy as it is pleasant ; but what proves clearly that it is difficult to succeed in it and bring it to perfection is that this title of *maître de ballet*, so lightly assumed, is only very rarely deserved.

Not one of them can excel, if he be not truly favoured by nature. What are our capabilities if they be not aided by genius, imagination and taste ? How can obstacles be overcome, difficulties smoothed away, the limits of mediocrity be passed, if there have not been planted in one the seed of one's art ?

Finally, if one be not gifted with all the talents which study can never confer, which cannot be acquired by use and which, inborn in the artist, are the forces which lend him wings and raise him at one flight to the summit of perfection and to the furthermost degree of his art—it is useless to adopt this calling.

If you consult Lucian,[1] you will learn from him, Sir, all the qualities which distinguish and characterise the true *maître de ballet*, and you will observe that history, fable, the

---

[1] A reference to περὶ ὀρχήσεως, *De Saltatione*, a disputation between Lucian and Crates, a stoic philosopher, concerning dancing. A translation of this work will be found in *The Works of Lucian of Samosata* (trs. by H. W. Fowler and F. G. Fowler, 4 vols., 1905), Vol. 2., p. 238 : *Of Pantomime*.

poems of antiquity and the knowledge of past times demand his whole application. In fact, it is only after an exact knowledge in all these spheres, that we can hope to succeed in our compositions. Let us unite the poet's genius and the painter's genius : the one to conceive, the other to execute.

An acquaintance with geometry cannot but be helpful : it will impart neatness to the figures, order to the combinations, precision to the forms and, in lessening moments of tedium, lend accuracy to the execution.

A ballet is a type of more or less complicated machinery, the different effects of which only impress and astonish in proportion as they follow in quick succession ; those combinations and sequences of figures, those movements which follow rapidly, those forms which turn in opposite ways, that mixture of *enchaînements*, that *ensemble*, and that harmony which presides over the steps and the various developments—do not all these afford you an idea of an ingeniously contrived machine ?

Cannot those ballets which, on the contrary, bring only disorder and confusion in their train, whose development is disjointed, whose figures are muddled, which betray the expectations of the artist and the anticipation of the public, because they err alike in a sense of proportion and accuracy, be compared to ill-arranged pieces of machinery, over-burdened with cogs and springs ?

Again, our productions often partake of the marvellous. Many of them require machinery ; for example, there are few themes taken from Ovid which can be represented without changes of scenery, flights, transformations, etc. Hence a *maître de ballet* cannot make use of subjects of this kind unless he himself be a machinist. Unfortunately, in the provinces, there can be found only casual labour or stage hands whom the patronage of some important actor has raised by degrees to this post ; their talents consist in, and are restricted to, the raising of chandeliers, the candles[1] of

[1] The stages of the theatres of the eighteenth century were illuminated by candelabra suspended over the stage and by foot-lights. These candles were generally snuffed during the intervals between the acts, since this could not be done during the progress of the play without detracting from its interest. The persons responsible for this work were known (in France) as *Moucheurs*, or snuffers. Generally, two were employed ; one for the front of the stage, and one for the back. The task of snuffing the candles required a certain dexterity, that the spectators

which they have been accustomed to snuff for many years, or
to the lowering by a series of jerks of an ill-arranged *gloire*.[1]

The theatres of Italy do not shine in their mechanical
equipment; those of Germany, constructed along similar
lines, are equally deficient in material for the production of
theatrical illusions; hence a *maître de ballet* would find himself
greatly at a loss in these theatres if he had not some knowledge of mechanics, if he could not explain his ideas clearly
and for this purpose construct little models, which are always
much better understood by workmen than all the talking
in the world, however clear and precise it may be.

The theatres of Paris and London are the best provided
with mechanical resources. The English are ingenious,
their stage machinery is much simpler than ours, and their
effects are as quick as they are subtle. With them, every
piece of mechanism is beautifully finished and of an admirable
delicacy, and the neatness, care and accuracy common to
the smallest details undoubtedly contribute greatly to their
speed and precision. It is principally in their pantomimes,
childish entertainments devoid of taste and interest, and
poor in plot, that masterpieces of mechanism are displayed.
It may be stated that this type of spectacle, produced at
enormous expense, is designed only for those eyes which
are shocked at nothing and that it would achieve little success
at our theatres where no other pleasantry is permitted
except it be governed by decency, delicacy and refinement,
and offend against neither morals nor good taste.

might not be annoyed either by the length of the process or by the
smell of burning wax. Finally, care was necessary in order to prevent
the naked flames being brought into contact with the scenery.

[1] A *gloire* (literally, *glory*) was a stage machine frequently employed
in the theatres of the latter half of the seventeenth, and throughout
the eighteenth century. It consisted of a light wooden framework,
masked by canvas or cardboard painted to represent a chariot or
cloud, in which, or on which, sat an actor or actress impersonating
a divinity such as Jupiter, Juno, Venus, Mercury, etc. This apparatus
was lowered, by stout ropes, from the "flies" to a short distance
below, where it remained in view of the audience. It was intended
to express the apparition of a supernatural being come to exert his or
her influence for good or evil at some critical moment in the ballet
or play: thus fulfilling a similar purpose to the *Deus ex machina* of
the ancient Greek theatre. Sometimes two or more *gloires* were
used at the same time. In the nineteenth century the *gloire* became
a complicated and very large framework used to support a group
of fairies to form an apotheosis in a spectacular ballet or in a

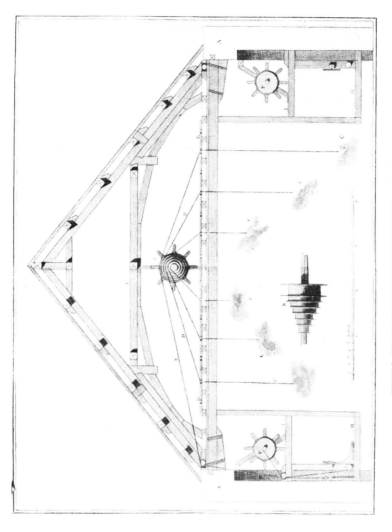

XVIIIth CENTURY STAGE EQUIPMENT: A GLOIRE
From Diderot & D'Alembert's "Encyclopédie," 1751–72

A composer who desires to rise above his fellows should study painters and copy them in their different methods of design and execution. Both arts have the same object in view, whether it be for the achieving of likeness, the admixture of colours, the play of light and shade, or the grouping and draping of figures, posing them in graceful attitudes and giving them character, life and expression; but now, how can a *maître de ballet* hope to succeed if he do not possess the abilities and qualities which go to the making of an eminent painter ?

Acting on this principle, I dare conclude that the study of anatomy will render clearer the precepts which he will impart to the pupils he wishes to train : from that moment he will distinguish with ease the natural and habitual defects of physique which so often impede a pupil's progress. Understanding the cause of the evil, he will easily remedy it; and, basing his lessons and counsels on a strict and careful examination, they cannot but be profitable. It is due to this lack of study of their pupils' physique, which varies as much as their physiognomies, that we owe that swarm of bad dancers which undoubtedly would be less numerous, if care had been taken to place them in a suitable calling.

M. Bourgelat,[1] the King's Riding-master and Director of the Riding Academy at Lyon, beloved as much by foreigners as by his own countrymen, was not content to train horses for the greater part of his life. He carefully studied their constitutions even to the smallest tendons. Do not assume that the diseases of these animals were the sole aim of his anatomical studies ; he has, as it were, compelled nature to reveal to him those secrets which hitherto had been constantly withheld. The intimate knowledge of the harmonic progress of the horse's limbs, in all its paces and under all conditions, as well as the discovery of the source, principle and means of all the movements of which the animal is capable, led him to a unique, simple and easy method which teaches one never to demand anything of one's mount except at the due, natural and possible time ; a time which is the

[1] Claude Bourgelat (1712-1779), a famous French veterinary surgeon who first made the treatment of animals a science. He was also the author of several works on the anatomy and diseases of domestic animals.

only one when the execution does not distress the animal and when it cannot escape obedience.

A painter does not study anatomy for the purpose of depicting skeletons : he does not make drawings after *The Flayed Man* of Michelangelo to place hideous forms in his pictures : however, these studies are imperative to enable him to render Man in all his proportions and portray him in all his movements and attitudes.

If the human form ought to be guessed at beneath the drapery, then the bones should be guessed at beneath the flesh.   It is essential to distinguish the place which each part should occupy ; the man must be under the drapery, the flayed body under the skin, and the skeleton under the flesh, if the figure is to be drawn in the true image of nature and in the correct proportions of art.

Drawing is too useful an art in the preparation of ballets for those who compose them not to study it seriously.   It will contribute to the charm of the forms, it will infuse novelty and elegance into the figures, voluptuousness into the groups, grace in the positions of the body, precision and truth in the attitudes.   The *maître de ballet* who neglects drawing will commit grave faults of composition.   The heads will no longer be posed agreeably and will contrast ill with the positions of the body, the arms will no longer be placed in easy attitudes ; the whole will be cumbersome, reveal the labour expended in the preparation of it, be disconnected and inharmonious.

The *maître de ballet* who ignores the study of music will ill-phrase the melodies and understand neither their spirit nor their character.   He will not combine the movements in the dance with the measure of the music with that precision and acuteness of hearing which are absolutely necessary, unless he be gifted with that sensitive ear which is more generally the gift of nature than the result of art, and which is far superior to that which may be acquired by study and practice.

The ability to select good music is as essential a part of dancing as the choice of words and the art of devising happy phrases is to eloquence.   It is the time and tone of the music which fix and determine all the dancer's movements. If the playing of the airs be expressionless and devoid of taste, the ballet, like its model, will be dull and uninteresting.

Owing to the intimate affinity between music and dancing, there can be no doubt, Sir, that a *maître de ballet* will derive marked advantage from a practical knowledge of this art. He will be able to communicate his thoughts to the composer, and, if he join a liking to knowledge, he will write the music himself or supply the composer with the principal ideas which should inspire his work ; these being expressive and varied the dance cannot fail to be so in its turn. Well-composed music should paint and speak : dancing, in imitating its sounds, will be the echo which will repeat everything it articulates. If, on the contrary, it be mute, it will tell the dancer nothing and he cannot respond to it : thence all feeling, all expression, is banished from the performance.

Since nothing comes amiss to genius, the same should hold good of a *maître de ballet*. He cannot distinguish himself in his profession unless he apply himself to the study of those arts which I have mentioned : to insist that he should possess them all in that high degree which is attained only by those who concentrate on one of them, would be asking the impossible ; but, if it cannot be so in practice, it should be so in theory.

I ask for a general knowledge only, a speaking acquaintance with every science and art which by their inter-relation can contribute to the embellishment and glory of our own.

The arts go hand in hand and may be compared to the members of a numerous family who seek to become illustrious : their usefulness to society excites their emulation, glory is their sole aim and they mutually aid each other to attain it. Each of them proceeds by different ways, for each has different principles ; but in each, however, one finds certain striking features, a certain resemblance which proves their intimate union and the need they have of each other for their mutual elevation, embellishment and continuation.

From this agreement of the arts, from this harmony which reigns over them, we may conclude, Sir, that the *maître de ballet* whose knowledge is the most extensive and who has the most genius and imagination will be he who invests his compositions with the most enthusiasm, truth, vitality and interest.

I am, &c.

LETTER VI

IF, Sir, the arts help one another, if they offer their assistance to dancing, nature seems eager to provide it at each moment with new resources ; the court and the village, the elements, the seasons, everything contributes to furnish it with means to be varied and to please.

A *maître de ballet*, then, ought to explore everything, to examine all, since everything that exists in the universe can serve him as a model.

How many varied pictures will he not find among work-men ! Each of them has different attitudes relative to the positions and movements exacted by his work. That gait, this deportment, that manner of always moving according to his trade—and always diverting—should be noted by the composer. It is easier to imitate these because the people of every trade are distinguished by certain indelible charac-teristics, which continue unaltered even if they have made a fortune and retired from business ; for they are the general effects of habits contracted over long periods and aggravated by fatigue and labour.

Again, what quaint and curious pictures will he not find in the crowd of pleasing idlers, those second-rate fops who ape and caricature the foibles of those upon whom age or fortune seem to confer the privilege of being frivolous, inconsequent and fatuous !

Crowded streets, public walks, tea gardens, rural pastimes and country occupations, a village wedding, hunting, fishing, the harvest and the vintage, a lover's mode of presenting a blossom to his lass, the rustic manner of watering a flower, of bird's-nesting and of playing on a reed-pipe, all will provide him with pictures as charming as they are varied and widely different in colour and character.

A camp, military drill and evolutions, the siege and

defence of fortresses, a seaport, a roadstead, an embarkation and a landing ; here are themes which attract our attention and bring our art to perfection, if the realisation be faithful.

Again, cannot the masterpieces of men like Racine, Corneille, Voltaire and Crébillon[1] serve as subjects for ballet in the grand style ? Do not those of Molière, Regnard[2] and many other celebrated authors provide us with themes of a less elevated kind ? I hear the dancing profession cry out at this proposal and designate me a madman : translate tragedies and comedies into dancing, what imbecility ! As if such a thing were possible ! Yes, undoubtedly : condense the plot of *L'Avare*, cut out all the quiet dialogue in the piece, bring the incidents together in closer relation, unite the scattered episodes, and you will succeed.

You will express quite clearly the scene of the ring, in which the miser searches his servant, La Flèche,[3] the one in which Frosine tells him of her mistress ;[4] you will depict Harpagon's despair and fury[5] in colours as brilliant as those used by Molière himself—if you have a soul at all. Everything that is of value in painting should be employed in dancing : if I can be persuaded that the works of the authors I have just mentioned are devoid of character and interest, present no striking situations and that a Boucher or a Vanloo[6] would never be able to devise from these masterpieces other than uninteresting and disagreeable pictures, I will admit that what I have submitted is nothing but a paradox ; but, if these pieces can provide the subjects for a number of excellent paintings, I have gained my suit, it is not my fault if we lack painters in pantomime and if genius does not exist among our dancers.

---

[1] Prosper Jolyot de Crébillon (1674-1762), a celebrated French playwright.

[2] Jean François Regnard (1655-1709), a popular French comic poet. He wrote a number of comedies of which *Le Joueur* (1696) is generally accounted the best.

[3] Act I, Scene iii.

[4] Act II, Scene vi.

[5] Act IV, Scene vii.

[6] Charles André or Carle Vanloo (1705-1765), an eminent French painter.

Did not Bathyllus, Pylades and Hylas[1] succeed the comedians when the latter were banished from Rome? Did they not commence to express in pantomime scenes from the best plays of their time? Encouraged by their successes, they attempted to play separate acts and their victory determined them finally to present whole plays, which were received with unanimous applause.

But these pieces, it will be argued, were well known. This knowledge served the spectators, as it were, in the same manner as a programme, since, knowing the plot by heart, they followed the mime without any difficulty, and even guessed beforehand what was coming. Shall we not possess the same advantage if we express in dancing the most esteemed dramas of our stage? Are we then not so skilful as the dancers of Rome, and is it not possible to perform to-day what was accomplished in the time of Augustus? It would be an insult to men of our age to think so, and to despise the taste and the intelligence of our days to believe it.

To return to the main point, a *maître de ballet* should be acquainted with both the beauties and the defects of nature. This study will enable him always to choose discriminately; besides, the pictures he creates being in turn historical, poetic, satirical, allegorical and moral, he will be obliged to take his models from all ranks, callings and conditions of society. If he had achieved fame, he would be able, through the magic and charm of his art, to execrate vice and reward virtue like the poet and the painter.

If a *maître de ballet* were to study nature and exercise a proper sense of selection, if the choice of subjects which he wished to express in dancing would contribute in a great measure to the success of his work, these would be dependent on his having the art and genius to embellish and present them in a grand and picturesque manner.

If, for instance, he wish to depict jealousy and all its succeeding moments of fury and despair, he will take as his model a man whose natural violence and brutality have been masked by a veneer of education; in a way, a porter would be a good enough model, but his appearance would

[1] A famous mime who achieved a great reputation at Rome in the time of Augustus. He was a pupil of Pylades.

not commend him to the audience; a stick in his hands would compensate for his lack of expression, but this representation, although taken from life, would disgust the spectators and exhibit a shocking picture of human imperfections. Besides, the actions of a jealous rag-picker would be less picturesque than those of a man of loftier feeling. The former will revenge himself on the spot by sheer strength of his arm : the latter, on the contrary, will struggle against the thoughts of a base and degrading vengeance. This inward contest between fury and high-minded feeling will lend strength and energy to his walk, demeanour, attitudes, features and looks ; everything will indicate his passion and reveal the state of his feelings. His self-imposed efforts at restraint, to moderate the movements by which he is tormented, will only serve to make them burst forth more violently than ever ; the more restrained his passion, the more violent will be its explosion, and the effect will be all the more pronounced.

The rude rustic can only afford a single gesture to the painter since, in his search for vengeance, he gains from its accomplishment but a low and worthless satisfaction. The man of breeding can, on the contrary, provide the painter with a multitude of pictures ; he expresses his passion and distress in a hundred different ways and always with both vigour and nobility. What diversity and contrast in his gestures ! What risings and fallings in his transports ! What varying shades of expression on his features ! What animation in his looks ! How expressive is his silence ! The moment when he finds his jealousy unfounded offers pictures more varied and more seductive still, and of a softer and more pleasing tone. These are the features that a *maître de ballet* ought to visualise instinctively.

Celebrated composers, just as illustrious poets and painters, always degrade themselves in wasting their time and genius on low and trivial productions. Great men should create only great things and leave puerilities to those inferior beings whose existence is ever ridiculous.

Nature does not always afford us models of perfection, hence one must possess the art of correcting them, of presenting them in a pleasing light, at an appropriate moment, in agreeable situations which, while veiling their defects, still confer on them the graces and charms which they ought to possess to be really beautiful.

The difficulty is, as I have remarked already, to embellish nature without marring her, to preserve all her features and to have the skill to soften or to strengthen them. The success of a picture depends on its being shown at the right moment which, by no means easy to seize upon, is still more difficult to render logical. Let us be guided by nature, for ever by nature, and our compositions will be beautiful. Away with art if it owe nothing to nature, if it be not embellished by her simplicity! Art captivates only in proportion as it is concealed, it does not succeed except it be so disguised as to be mistaken for nature herself.

I am of the opinion, Sir, that a *maître de ballet* who does not possess a complete knowledge of dancing can compose in a mediocre manner only. By dancing, I mean the serious style which is the true foundation of ballets. If he ignore its principles his resources will be limited, he must renounce the grand style, abandon history, mythology and national dances, and confine himself solely to ballets founded on peasant dances with which the public is surfeited and wearied since the arrival of Fossan, that excellent comic dancer who introduced into France the rage for high jumping. I compare fine dancing to a mother tongue, and the mixed and degenerate style derived from it to those rough dialects which can be hardly understood, and which vary in proportion to the distance from the capital where the language is spoken in its greatest purity.

The combination of colours, their gradations and their effect under artificial light should also occupy the attention of the *maître de ballet*. I have learned by experience the heightening effect which they give to figures, the sharpness of form they induce and the elegance they accord to the groups. In *Les Jalousies, ou les Fêtes du Sérail*, I paid attention to the degrees of light and shade such as painters observe in their pictures; strong, primary colours came first and then quieter and less brilliant tones. I retained the soft and misty hues for the background. The executants were graduated in the same manner according to their heights. The performance gained greatly by this careful arrangement. Everything was in harmony and at peace;

nothing clashed ; this unison enchanted the vision which took in every detail without fatigue.

This ballet had a greater success than the other I called *Ballet Chinois* which I revived at Lyon ; the ill-arranged colours and their disagreeable combination hurt the eyes, all the figures dazzled and confused the spectator, although the ballet was correctly planned ; in fact, nothing achieved the effect it ought to have done. The dresses killed, so to speak, the production, because their colours resembled too closely those of the scenery ; everything was splendid, all the colours were brilliant, everything glittered with the same gaudiness ; no part was subordinate to another and this uniformity in all the details deprived the picture of its effect, because there was no contrast, the wearied eye of the spectator could distinguish nothing. That multitude of dancers who trailed after them tawdry tinsel and that fantastic conglomeration of colours dazzled the eyes without satisfying them.

The effect of the costumes was such that the wearer could no longer be distinguished the moment he ceased to move, yet this ballet was rendered with all possible precision ; the beauty of the theatre gave it an elegance and a sharpness of outline which it would not have obtained at Paris in M. Monnet's[1] theatre ; but whether the costumes and scenery were not in harmony, or whether the style I have now adopted be superior to that I rejected, I am forced to admit that of all my ballets it is the one which has made the least sensation.

The gradation of the dancers' heights and the colours of their dresses is unknown to our stage ; nor is this the only thing that has been neglected : but this inattention seems to be inexcusable in certain circumstances, above all at the *Opéra*, the realm of fancy ; the theatre where painting should display all its treasures, the theatre at which the representations are so often devoid of strong action and lively interest, when they should be rich in pictures of all styles.

A scene of any kind is a large picture awaiting the painting in of the figures. The actresses and actors, the *danseurs* and

---

[1] Jean Monnet (1710-1785), a French dramatic author. He was director of the Opéra Comique (1743), then director of a theatre at Lyon (1745), and again director of the Opéra Comique until 1757.

danseuses, are the personages who should adorn and embellish it, but in order that the picture shall please and not offend the sight, a just proportion must reign equally over all the different parts of which it is composed.

If, in a scene representing a temple or a palace in blue and gold, the dresses of the actors be of the same colours, they will destroy the effect of the scenery and this, in its turn, will deprive the costumes of the splendour they would have had when set against a quieter background. Such a disposition of the colours will spoil the whole picture so that it will be similar to a cameo, and this monotonous effect will soon fatigue the eye and transmit its uniformity and coldness to the action. The colours of the draperies and of the costumes should contrast with those of the scenery, which I compare to a beautiful background. If the latter be not restful, it is inharmonious : if the colours be too vivid and too brilliant, it will deprive the figures of the relief that they should have ; nothing will stand out because nothing will be arranged artistically, and the gaudy effect which will result from the clashing of the colours will present but a panel of cut-out figures lighted up without taste or intelligence.

In scenes of a chaste beauty and containing few colours, rich and striking dresses can be employed as well as those slashed with brilliant and primary colours.

In fanciful and tasteful scenes such as: *A Chinese Palace* or *A Public Square in Constantinople*, decorated for a festival, such a fantastic style, not subject to strict rules, affords a wide scope to the painter, so that the success of the scene is in proportion to the originality of his treatment. In such scenes, I repeat, radiant with colour and hung with stuffs heightened with gold and silver, the costumes must be simple and their colour values completely contrasted with those hues that are most prominent in the scenery. If this rule be not strictly maintained, the whole effect will be marred for lack of shade and contrast. On the stage everything must be in harmony. When scenery is designed with an eye to the costumes and *vice versa*, the charm of representation will be complete.

Persons of taste and, above all, artists will appreciate the logic and importance of this observation.

The gradation of the heights of the dancers must be observed no less scrupulously whenever dances form part of the decorative scheme. Olympus and Parnassus are among the places represented when the ballet is responsible for three-quarters of the effect, but such scenes can neither captivate nor charm unless the scenic artist and the *maître de ballet* collaborate in regard to the proportions, disposition and attitudes of the performers.

Is it not ridiculous and disgraceful that in a theatre so well appointed as the *Opéra* no attempt is made to graduate the performers according to their heights, when the laws of perspective are rigidly adhered to in the scenery, which after all is subsidiary to the complete picture ? Jupiter on the pinnacle of Olympus, or Apollo placed on the summit of Parnassus, should surely, on account of their distance from the audience, appear smaller than the lesser gods and muses who, being placed lower down, are nearer ? If, in order to create a sense of illusion, the scenic artist work in accordance with the laws of perspective, why should the *maître de ballet*, who is likewise an artist, or should be, transgress them ? How can these pictures please, if they be not lifelike, if they be devoid of proportion, if they set aside the principles which art acquired from nature by a comparison of the size of objects ? It is particularly in fixed and stationary scenes in a ballet that gradation should be used, even if it be not so important in those scenes which arise naturally during the progress of the dances. When I speak of fixed pictures, I mean all those dancers grouped at a distance who merge into the background and form with it a well-ordered scheme.

But, you will say to me, how is this grading to be carried out ? Suppose a Vestris dances the part of Apollo, must the ballet be deprived of so great a talent and sacrifice all the charm he could contribute to it, for the pleasure of a moment ? Certainly not, but, for such a moment, one would take an Apollo adapted to the scheme, a young man of some fifteen years who could be dressed like the Apollo who is to dance. He would come down from Parnassus to disappear behind one of the " wings ", when his place would be taken by the elegant and superior talent of the dancer.

It is owing to such continual experiments that I am convinced of the admirable effects produced by grading.

My first attempt, which was successful, was made in a ballet of huntsmen, and this idea, perhaps new to the art of ballet, arose from the impression made upon me by a gross fault committed by M. Servandoni, a fault due to carelessness which did not reflect on his reputation as an artist; it occurred, I believe, in the beautiful production called *La Forêt Enchantée*, founded on a theme taken from Tasso. A bridge was set far back on the right-hand side of the stage, and across this a number of persons defiled; each one of them appeared of an enormous stature and seemed larger than the whole of the bridge; the counterfeit horses were smaller than their riders; and these faults in proportion offended even the most unpractised eye. This bridge might have been in correct proportion to the scenery, but it was not so in relation to the human beings who passed across it, hence they should have been either eliminated or replaced by smaller persons: such, for instance, as children mounted on counterfeit horses proportionate both to them and to the bridge, which, in this case, was the part which should have been arranged and determined by the scenic artist in order to have produced the most pleasing and most realistic effect.

I tried then, in a hunting scene, to achieve what I had wished to see in M. Servandoni's production. The scenery represented a forest, the roads of which ran parallel to the spectator. In the background was a bridge beyond which a distant landscape could be seen. I divided the procession into six classes, each carefully graded. Each class consisted of three horsemen and three horsewomen, which together made up a total of thirty-six persons. The first and tallest class passed along the road nearest to the spectator, those of the second followed on the next road, and those of the third followed along the third road, and so on, up to the final class composed of little children who crossed the last road and passed over the bridge. The grading was so precisely arranged that the eye was deceived: so that what was only the result of art and perspective had the most realistic and natural appearance. The illusion was such that the public attributed the gradation to the distance of the objects, and imagined that it was always the same horsemen and horsewomen who crossed by the different roads in the forest. The sounds of the music were similarly graduated, and became fainter as the hunt went deeper into the vast forest, which was well depicted.

I cannot tell you the pleasure which this idea, when carried out, afforded me. The result exceeded all my expectations and was universally applauded.

This, Sir, is the illusion produced on the stage when the details of the production are in harmony, and when artists take nature as their guide and model.

I think that I shall have almost fulfilled the object of this letter when I have made just one more observation on the harmony of colours. *Les Jalousies, ou Les Fêtes du Sérail* has afforded you a sketch of the distribution which ought to take place in the quadrilles of ballets. But, as it is more usual to dress the dancers alike, I have made a successful experiment which takes away from the uniformity of the costumes their hard and monotonous effect. This consists in the exact grading of the same colour divided up into all its different shades, from dark blue to the lightest blue, from carmine to pale pink, from dark purple to pale lilac. This arrangement gives play and sharpness to the figures, everything stands out in the right proportion, and is seen clearly against the background.

If, in a scene representing a cave of Hell, the *maître de ballet* desire that the raising of the curtain should reveal this terrible spot and the torments of the Danaïdes, Ixion, Tantalus and Sisyphus, and the different pursuits of the infernal gods : if he wish to show at the first glance a moving and terrifying picture of the tortures of Hell ; how will he succeed in this instantaneous effect if he have not the talent of disposing objects and arranging them in the place proper to each, if he have not the talent of seizing the first idea of the painter and subordinating his own to the scenery which the former has designed for him ?

He will see dark rocks and luminous rocks, obscure parts and parts gleaming with fire. A well-ordered horror should reign in the tomb; everything should be awe-inspiring; everything should indicate the place of the scene and display the torments and tortures of those who inhabit it. Dwellers in Hell, as they are represented on the stage, are clothed in flame-coloured garments; sometimes the ground of their dress is black, sometimes poppy-coloured or bright red ; all the hues are borrowed from the scenery. The *maître de ballet* should see that the lightest and most brilliant dresses are placed in the dark portions of the scenery, and distribute the darker costumes against the light-coloured masses. From this careful arrangement harmony will arise. The scenery will serve, if I may so express myself, as a contrast to the ballet; the latter in its turn will increase the charm of the scenery and endow it with the power to attract, to move and to deceive the spectator.

I am, &c.

WHAT is your opinion, Sir, of all those titles daily bestowed upon those sorry entertainments destined in some manner to induce boredom and for ever provoking indifference and disgust ? They are called *ballets-pantomimes*, although in reality they express nothing. Dancers and composers have need, for the most part, to adopt the practice followed by painters in the dark ages. In place of masks, they made use of scrolls of paper which issued from the mouths of their characters ; and these scrolls were inscribed with the action, expression and situation necessary to each. This useful precaution rendered intelligible to the spectator the purport of the representation which, otherwise, owing to the painter's lack of skill, would have remained incomprehensible ; this procedure might well be applied for the purpose of explaining the mechanical and uncertain movements in our pantomimes of to-day. The dialogue expressed in a *pas de deux*, the soliloquies indicated in a *pas seul*, and the conversations represented by the *corps de ballet* would nowadays at least be understood.

A nosegay, a rake, a cage, a hurdy-gurdy or a guitar, there you have almost all the objects about which revolve the plots of our superb ballets—such are the sources of the grand and mighty themes born of our composers' imaginations ! You must confess, Sir, that to treat such subjects in a fitting manner demands a talent of unusual eminence and superiority. A clumsy *petit battement sur le cou de pied* serves alike as introduction, plot and climax to these masterpieces ; it implies, " Will you dance with me ? " and the dance takes place. These are the ingenious dramas with which we are surfeited ; these are what are termed original ballets expressed in pantomimic dancing.

Fossan, the most pleasing and most witty of all comic

dancers, has turned the heads of the votaries of Terpsichore ;
everyone wished to copy him, some even without having
seen him. The noble style was sacrificed to the trivial, the
principles of the art were set aside, all rules were disdained
and rejected, high jumps and feats of strength became the
order of the day. Dancers ceased to dance and believed
themselves capable of pantomime ; as if such a thing were
possible when the power of expression was completely
lacking, when nothing could be represented, when dancing
was disfigured by coarse caricatures, subjected to hideous
contortions, when the mask grimaced beyond all reason ;
finally, when action, which should be accompanied and
sustained by grace, was a continual repetition of a series of
effects, rendered the more disagreeable to the spectator in
that he himself suffered from witnessing the painful labours
and strained efforts of the dancer. And yet, Sir, such is the
style of dancing predominant on our stage to-day ; and it
must be admitted that we are rich in productions of this
kind. This mad passion to imitate that which is inimitable
proves, and will prove, the downfall of an infinite number of
dancers and *maîtres de ballet*. A perfect imitation demands
the possession of precisely the same taste, disposition,
physique, intelligence and organs as the person it is proposed to imitate. Now it is rare to find two persons alike
in facial appearance and physical proportion, it is rarer still
to discover two men whose talents, tastes and manners
exactly correspond.

The practice introduced by dancers of employing *cabrioles*
in the noble style of dancing has altered its character and
deprived it of its dignity. It forms an alloy which lowers the
worth of dancing and impedes, as I shall presently prove, the
lively expression and animated action which it should possess,
if it were able to disembarrass itself of the futilities falsely
included among its perfections. It is only nowadays that
the title of ballet has been applied to those figure dances
which should be called *divertissements ;* in former times the
name of ballet was lavishly bestowed on all the splendid
festivals given at the different Courts of Europe.

The examination I have made of all these festivals has
persuaded me that the title of ballet accorded them was a
misnomer. I have never seen in them a *danse d'action ;*

long recitatives were introduced in order to acquaint the spectator with what the performance was intended to convey —a very clear and convincing proof of their incompetence, as well as of the complete insignificance and lack of expression in their movements.

As far back as the third century the monotony of the art of dancing and the carelessness of the dancers was perceived and commented upon. Saint Augustine himself, in speaking of ballets, remarked that a man was invariably placed on the edge of the stage, to explain in a loud voice the action about to be represented. In the reign of Louis XIV, recitatives, dialogues and monologues equally served as an explanation of the dancing which could not yet speak for itself. Its feeble and inarticulate sounds had need to be supported by music and explained by poetry, and these are undoubtedly equivalent to that kind of herald of the theatre, the public crier I have mentioned. It is truly astonishing, Sir, that such a glorious epoch of the triumph of the fine arts and of the friendly rivalry of artists should not have contributed to a similar revolution in dancing and ballets ; and that our *maîtres de ballet*, no less encouraged and excited by the promise of success in an age when everything seemed to conspire to raise and favour genius, should have remained sunk in languor and a shameful inefficiency.

You are well aware that then painting, poetry and sculpture expressed themselves in terms of eloquence and energy. Music, though still in its infancy, began to express itself with dignity ; dancing, however, continued lifeless, devoid of character and action. If ballet is to be accounted brother to the other arts, this relationship is dependent on its possessing all their characteristics, and it can hardly be considered worthy of this glorious designation having regard to its present pitiful condition. You must admit, Sir, that this brother, created to bring honour to his family, is a wretched being without taste, wit or imagination, who merits, in every respect, complete disavowal.

We are perfectly acquainted with the names of the illustrious men of that period ; neither do we ignore even those acrobatic dancers who distinguished themselves by virtue of their suppleness and agility ; but we have only a very inadequate knowledge of the names of those who composed ballets : what opinion, then, can we form of their talents ?

I consider all productions of this type given at the different Courts of Europe to have been but feeble shadows of what they are now and of what they can some day become. I am of the opinion, then, that the name of ballet has been wrongly applied to such sumptuous entertainments, such splendid festivals which combine magnificent scenery, wonderful machinery, rich and pompous costumes, charming poetry, music and declamation, seductive voices, brilliant artificial illumination, pleasing dances and *divertissements*, thrilling and perilous jumps, and feats of strength: all of which parts when separated form as many different spectacles, but when united form one complete entertainment worthy of the most powerful monarch.

These festivals were the more pleasing according as they were the more varied, so that each spectator could find something to his own taste and fancy, but even in all this I discover nothing of what I seek to find in a ballet. Setting aside all enthusiasm and professional prejudice, I consider this complicated entertainment as one of variety and magnificence, or as an intimate union of the pleasing arts wherein each holds an equal rank which they should similarly occupy in the production as a whole. Nevertheless, I do not see how the title of ballet can be accorded to those *divertissements* which are not *danses d'action*, which express nothing and are superior in no way to the other arts, each of which contributes to the elegance and wonder of these representations.

According to Plutarch, a ballet is a conversation in dumb show, a speaking and animated picture which expresses all in terms of movement, groups and gestures. These groupings are innumerable, declares this author, because a ballet can express an infinity of things. Phrynicus, one of the oldest tragic authors, asserts that he could find in a ballet as many different figures and manifestations as the sea has waves in the great floods of winter.

Consequently, a well-planned ballet can dispense with the aid of words. I have even remarked that they chill the action and weaken the interest. When dancers are animated by their feelings, they will assume a thousand different

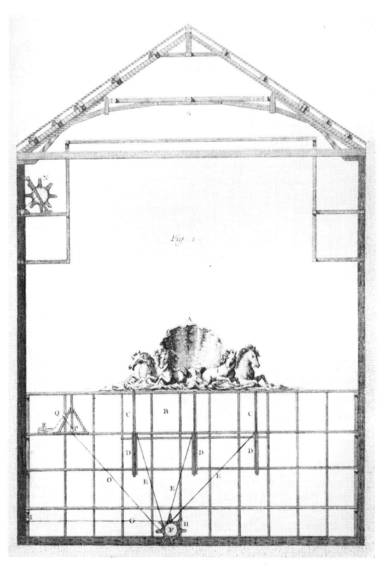

XVIIITH CENTURY STAGE EQUIPMENT
Device used to produce the effect of Neptune's chariot rising from the waves
From Diderot & D'Alembert's "Encyclopédie," 1751-72

attitudes according to the varied symptoms of their passions ; when, Proteus-like, their features and glances betray the conflicts in their breast, when their arms break through the limited movements prescribed by the laws of technique, to move with grace and judgment in every direction, they will express in their appropriate positions the successive stages of their passions.

Finally, when they bring thought and genius to their art, they will become distinguished. Words will become useless, everything will speak, each movement will be expressive, each attitude will depict a particular situation, each gesture will reveal a thought, each glance will convey a new sentiment ; everything will be captivating, because all will be a true and faithful imitation of nature.

If I withhold the title of ballet from all these festivals, if the majority of the dances presented at the *Opéra*, however agreeable they may appear to me, do not convey to my eyes the distinctive features of a ballet, it is less the fault of the celebrated *maître de ballet* who composed them than that of the poets.

According to Aristotle, a ballet, like poetry, of whatever style, should contain two different parts, that of quality and that of quantity. Nothing exists without matter, form and figure, so that a ballet ceases to exist, if it do not include those essential parts characteristic of all things, whether animate or inanimate. Its matter is the theme which it is desired to represent, its form is the ingenuity of the plot given to it, and its figure is the different parts of which it is composed. Form therefore corresponds to quality, and extent to quantity.

Here, then, as you see, are ballets subordinated in some degree to the laws of poetry ; however, they differ from tragedies and comedies in that they are not subject to unity of place, time and action ; but they demand absolute unity of design, so that all the scenes converge and lead to the same end. Ballet then is brother to poetry, it cannot support the restraint of the narrow rules of drama ; those factors which genius imposes on works sustained by beauties of style, would completely disintegrate the composition of the ballet and deprive it of that variety wherein lies its charm. Perhaps it would be an advantage, Sir, to authors, to shake off the yoke a little and lessen the constraint, always provided that they had the wisdom not to abuse their liberty and to avoid the snares which it sets for the imagination, dangerous snares which even the most celebrated English poets have not had the strength to escape.

This difference between a poem and a drama affords nothing contrary to what I have remarked in my other letters, since these two kinds of poetry ought equally to possess an introduction, plot and climax.

In bringing together all my ideas, in collecting what early writers have remarked on ballets, in reviewing my art, in examining all its difficulties, in considering what it was formerly, what it is to-day, and what it may be, if intelligence comes to its aid, I cannot shut my eyes to the point of admitting that dancing without action, without rules, without intelligence, and without interest forms a ballet, or a poem expressed in terms of dancing. To say that there are no ballets at the *Opéra* would be a falsehood. The act of *Les Fleurs*, the act of Eglé in *Les Talents Lyriques*,[1] the prologue to *Les Fêtes Grecques et Romaines*,[2] the Turkish act in *l'Europe Galante*,[3] one act among many from *Castor et Pollux*,[4] and a quantity of others where dancing is, or can be, easily united to action, and without any extraordinary effort on the composer's part, truly offer me agreeable and very

[1] *Les Fêtes d'Hébé ou Les Talents Lyriques.* Ballet by Mondorge with music by Rameau. It was first performed on May 21st, 1739. In the revival of 1764, the part of *Eglé* was both danced and sung by Mlle. Guimard.

[2] An heroic ballet in three acts and a prologue. The words are by Fuzelier, the music by Colin de Blâmont. This ballet was first performed on July 13th, 1723. The three *entrées* in the ballet are *Jeux Olympiques*, *Bacchanales* and *Saturnales*. Mlle. Camargo played the part of *Terpsichore* with considerable success. When the ballet was revived in 1762 and 1770, this character was sustained by Mlle. Guimard.

[3] An opera-ballet in four acts. The words are by La Motte, the music by Campra. It was first performed at the Académie Royale de Musique on October 24th, 1697. In the revival of 1766, Mlle. Guimard played the part of a Sultana in the Turkish act.

[4] A lyric tragedy in five acts and a prologue. Poem by Gentil Bernard, music by Rameau. It was first presented at the Académie Royale de Musique on October 24th, 1737, when Mlle. Sallé took the part of *Hébé*. In the revivals of 1764, 1772, 1773 and 1778, Mlle. Guimard appeared as the *Happy Shadow*.

interesting ballets ; but those figure dances which express nothing, which present no story, which have no character, which do not sketch for me a connected and logical plot, which possess nothing dramatic and which fall, as it were, from the skies, are only, in my opinion, as I have remarked already, simple dancing *divertissements* which merely display the limited movements and mechanical difficulties of the art.   All this is simply matter ; it is gold, if you will, but the value of which is always limited, if intelligence be not bestowed on the production to afford it a thousand new forms.   The skilful hand of the artist can cause an inestimable price to be placed on the most worthless things, and with a bold stroke apply to the commonest clay the seal of immortality.

Let us conclude, Sir, that there are few logical ballets, that dancing is a beautiful statue pleasantly designed, that it is distinguished equally for its contours, its graceful positions and the nobility of its attitudes, but that it lacks a soul. Connoisseurs regard it as Pygmalion regarded his masterpiece.   They express the same wishes as he, and ardently desire it to be animated by feeling, to be lit up by genius and to be taught to express itself intelligently.

I am, &c.

LETTER VIII

THE composition of ballets which are to form part of an opera demands, in my opinion, Sir, a fertile and poetic imagination. The duty of a *maître de ballet* consists in adapting the poems to his purpose, joining dancing with action, imagining dramatic scenes and skilfully fitting them to the theme, devising those incidents which have escaped the poet's genius, and strengthening the weaknesses which so often detract from his productions ; such are the objects on which he should concentrate his attention in order to distinguish himself from those *maîtres de ballet* who fondly imagine that they have reached the summit of their profession when they have arranged a few steps and devised figures the design of which is limited to circles, squares, straight lines, " hands across " and " rights and lefts." Opera is intended for the eyes and ears alone, and makes little appeal to the heart or mind except as a means of variety or amusement. It might, however, be accorded a more interesting form and character, but, since such a discussion is foreign to my purpose, I leave it to those ingenious authors who can discover an antidote for the tedious similarity of the Fairy Tale and for the depression occasioned by continual recourse to the supernatural. I shall content myself with the observation that, in this type of representation, dancing should occupy a more prominent place. I will submit that opera is dancing's natural element and that as a result of this association dancing should acquire new strength and appear to the best advantage, but, owing to a misfortune born of the obstinacy of our poets, or the inefficiency of our *maîtres de ballet*, the part taken by the dance in an opera is such that the former is meaningless, contributes nothing to its effect and has no bearing on its theme. In fact, a thousand examples could be cited where dancing has so little connection with the plot and is so independent of the drama that it could be suppressed without weakening the interest, without interrupting the progress of the scenes and without chilling the action.

Most of our modern poets make use of ballets as a fanciful ornament which can neither sustain the play itself nor add to its merit. And, in truth, they are not wrong, because *maîtres de ballet* have not felt the necessity for ballets to be related to the theme, and authors have regarded them as little extras to fill in the intervals between the acts. But they should have perceived that these extras and these episodes, being foreign to the action, spoil the whole. These opposed and unrelated objects, this chaos of unconnected episodes, divide the spectator's attention and tire the imagination much more than they satisfy it. Hence the author's work becomes disconnected, the thread snaps, the woof is broken, the action vanishes, interest diminishes and pleasure takes to flight. As long as the ballets in an opera are not closely united with the theme and do not contribute to its introduction, plot and climax, they will be cold and displeasing. In my opinion, each ballet should present an attractive scene which provides a close bond between the first and second acts, the second and third, and so on. These scenes, absolutely necessary to the progress of the piece, would be lively and animated ; the dancers would be compelled to abandon their usual steps and to acquire a soul to render them with truth and precision. They would be compelled to forget, in some degree, their feet and think of their facial expression and gestures. Each ballet would be contributory to the act and round it off adroitly. These ballets, based on the very essence of the drama, would be composed by the poet ; the composer would faithfully render them in terms of music and the dancers would express them forcibly in gesture. By this means there would be no more gaps, futilities, waits and dull moments in the dances of an opera ; everything would be attractive and animated, everything would contribute to a concerted climax, everything would be captivating because of its wit and would appear to better advantage. In short, the illusion would be complete and therefore interesting, because the strictest harmony would prevail throughout, and each part, being in its proper place, would mutually aid and strengthen the others.

I have always regretted, Sir, that Rameau[1] did not collaborate with Quinault.[2] Both endowed with creative genius, they were made for each other ; but prejudice, the remarks of ignorant connoisseurs, of those pseudo-scholars who know nothing but sway the multitude, all this disgusted Rameau and led him to abandon the great ideas he had in mind. Added to this were the annoyances which every author experiences from the directors of the *Opéra*. To those gentry an author is devoid of taste unless he cling to the same ancient tenets as their own. It is a profanation, with them, not to follow blindly the old laws and ancient rubrics which have been handed down from father to son.

A *maître de ballet* is hardly permitted to alter the time of an old melody, it is quite useless for him to point out that our predecessors favoured a simple manner of execution and that a melody in slow time was thus fitted for their grave and solemn dances ; they understand the old ways, they know how to beat time, but their hearing does not stimulate their imagination. They concede nothing despite the materially improved condition of the art, they look at everything from the point at which they left off and cannot realise the immense progress which dancers have made since their hey-day.

The art of dancing, however, encouraged, praised and protected, has for some time past freed itself from the limitations which music sought to impose upon it. M. Lany[3] has not only rendered airs consonant with good taste, but has added new ones to the old operas and substituted pieces full of expression and variety for Lully's[4] simple and

[1] Jean Philippe Rameau (1683-1764), a celebrated French composer and writer on music. He composed more than twenty operas, including *Dardanus*, *Castor et Pollux* and *Les Indes Galantes*.

[2] Philippe Quinault (1635-1688), a French dramatic poet. His operas were set to music by Lully.

[3] Jean Barthélemy Lany (1718-1786), a celebrated French dancer and one of the best *maîtres de ballet* at the Académie Royale de Musique.

[4] Jean Baptiste Lully (*c.* 1639-1687), a famous Italian composer and musician. He was director of music to Louis XIV and director of the Paris Opéra. He composed the music for a number of opera-ballets and introduced dance music of a rapid rhythm in opposition to the slow and stately measures that had formerly prevailed. In December, 1661, he was naturalised as a Frenchman, his original name being Giovanni Battista Lulli.

monotonous songs.   In this respect the Italians have been wiser than we.   Less partial to their ancient music, but more faithful to Metastasio,[1] they have caused the works of that poet to be set to music by their most talented composers. The courts of Germany, Spain, Portugal and England have retained the same veneration for that great poet ; the music varies infinitely and the words, although the same, have always the attraction of novelty, because each composer accords the poet's words a new meaning and a new grace. One will embellish a sentiment overlooked by another, the thought weakened by that one is given full expression by this one, a beautiful verse spoilt by Graun[2] is expressed with enthusiasm by Hasse.[3]

There is no question of the advantage that would have been gained, not only by the dance but by all the other arts which contribute to the charm and perfection of opera, could the celebrated Rameau (without offending the sages of the century and that crowd of people who can conceive nothing superior to Lully) have set to music the master-pieces of the father and creator of lyric poetry.   This man, of a vast genius, combines everything in his works, all is beautiful, grand and harmonious.   Every artist in sympathy with the author can produce different masterpieces.   Com-posers, *maîtres de ballet*, singers, dancers, and choruses can equally share his fame.   It must be admitted that in Quin-ault's operas the dances are not always well placed, nor are they contributory to the theme, but it would be easy to improve what the poet has neglected and to complete what, from his point of view, are only intended to be rough sketches.

Even if my opinion bring down upon me the wrath of a multitude of old people, I shall assert that Lully's dance music is cold, tedious and devoid of character.   It is true that it was composed at a time when dancing was restrained

---

[1] Pietro Bonaventura Trapassi (1698-1787), better known by his assumed name of Metastasio, an eminent Italian poet.

[2] Karl Heinrich Graun (1701-1759), a celebrated German composer. In 1740 he was appointed *kapellmeister* to Frederick the Great.

[3] Johann Adolf Hasse (1699-1783), an eminent German composer who wrote a number of operas, the words for which were written by Metastasio.

and the executants totally ignored expression. Everything then was wonderful, the music was composed for the dance and *vice versa*. But what was compatible then is no longer so ; the steps are multiplied, the movements are quick and follow each other in rapid succession, there are an infinity of *enchaînements* and variations of time ; the difficulties, the sparkle, the speed, the indecisions, the attitudes, the diverse positions—all this, I say, cannot be harmonised with the grave music and uniform intonation which are the characteristics of the works of the old composers. The dances arranged to certain airs composed by Lully produced on me the same effect as the scene between the two doctors in Molière's *Le Mariage Forcé*.[1] This contrast between an extreme volubility and obstinate taciturnity are so completely opposed that they are out of place on the stage ; they destroy charm and proportion and spoil the picture as a whole.

Music is to dancing what words are to music; this parallel simply means that dance music corresponds, or should do, to the written poem and thus fixes and determines the dancer's movements and actions. He must therefore recite it and render it intelligible by the force and vivacity of his gestures, by the lively and animated expression of his features; consequently dancing with action is the instrument, or organ, by which the thoughts expressed in the music are rendered appropriately and intelligibly.

Nothing seems to me so stupid as an opera without words, you may prove this by the scene of Antoninus Caracalla in the little piece at the *Nouveautés ;* were it not for the prologue, who would understand the singer's gestures ? Well, dancing without music is no more intelligible than singing without words. It is a kind of madness which makes all the movements exaggerated and meaningless. To make bold and brilliant steps, to traverse the stage with speed and lightness to the accompaniment of a cold and dreary melody —that is what I call a dance without music.

The varied and harmonious compositions of Rameau, so full of wit and expression, are the cause of the recent improvement in dancing which has awakened it from the lethargy into which it was plunged. This happened from the moment that this clever creator of pleasing, yet ever volup-

[1] Scenes iv. and v.

tuous, music appeared on the scene. What would we not have achieved if the practice of mutual collaboration had been in force in opera, if the poet and *maître de ballet* had communicated their ideas to him, if they had taken the pains to outline to him the action of the dance, the passions it should portray successively in a logical theme and the scenes it should depict in certain situations. Then the music would have borne the likeness of a poem, it would have expressed the poet's thoughts, made itself intelligible, and the dancer would have been forced to grasp its inner meaning, build upon it and present the result to the public. The harmony which would have reigned between arts so closely allied would have produced the most admirable and capti-vating effect ; but, owing to an unfortunate conceit, artists, so far from consulting one another, take the greatest pains to avoid such a collaboration. How can a spectacle, so diversely constituted as that of opera, succeed, if those in charge of the different parts which compose it work without interchange of their ideas ? The poet is convinced that his art raises him far above the musical composer, the latter feels it beneath his dignity to consult the *maître de ballet ;* he, in turn, holds no communication with the scene-painter, who himself only speaks to his subordinates ; while the machinist, often despised by the painter, is in supreme command of the stage hands. If only the poet would treat others as his equals he would pave the way and things would soon alter for the better. But he listens only to his inspirations and, disdain-ing the other arts, can have but a superficial knowledge of them ; he ignores the effect which each of them can produce by itself and those which would result from their harmonious combination.

The musician, in turn, takes the libretto which he hurriedly peruses and then, determined to rely on his own resources of invention, composes a score which is meaningless, because he has not taken the trouble to understand what he has merely skimmed with his eyes. Or else, sacrificing every-thing in order to flatter his own vanity, he produces music entirely unrelated to the theme. Suppose an overture is required. What does it matter whether it be relative to the action about to be presented ? After all, is he not sure of success so long as it makes a sensation ? Melodies suitable for dances are still less trouble to compose, for in this case the composer follows old models; his predecessors are his guides; he does not take the slightest trouble to introduce a little variety into these kinds of pieces in order to give them an appearance of novelty. The monotonous chant which he should beware of, since it enervates the dancing and sends the spectator to sleep, is the very one which captivates him since it is the easiest to compose, and the servile imitation of old melodies demands neither taste, talent nor a superior genius. The scenic artist, instead of making it his business to understand the drama thoroughly, generally falls into error. He never consults the author, but follows his own devices, which, often false, are opposed to what the scenery should represent in order to indicate the place of action. How can he succeed if he know not what is required of him? He should not even begin his work until he has definite knowledge of the action and the place in which it is to occur. If this precaution be unheeded there can be neither truth, nor appropriate surroundings, nor any sense of the picturesque.

Every nation has its own laws, customs, manners, fashions and ceremonies, which are entirely different from those of another. Each nation differs in its tastes, architecture and mode of cultivating the arts. A skilful painter then should be able to seize on the different characteristics and depict them with a faithful brush. If he be not a cosmopolitan he cannot be true and he is no longer in a position to please.

The costume designer consults no one in regard to his dresses, and often sacrifices the correct costumes of the people of a bygone age to the fashion of the day or at the caprice of a favourite dancer or singer.

The *maître de ballet* is acquainted with no particulars, he is given the score and composes dances to the music provided. He distributes particular steps and afterwards the costumes give the dance its name and character.

The machinist is charged with the duty of presenting the scenic artist's pictures in their proper perspective and in the different lights requisite to them. His first care is to place the various pieces of scenery so that they form a complete and harmonious whole. His skill lies in accomplishing this with dispatch and dismantling the whole with equal celerity.

If he know not how to arrange the lighting, he spoils the painter's work and destroys the effect of the scenery. That portion of the picture which should be well lighted becomes dark and obscure, another part which should be shrouded in gloom is clear and brilliant. It is not the great number of lamps, distributed at chance or symmetrically arranged, which lights up the stage and sets off the scenery ; the skill consists in knowing how to distribute the lights, or mass them in unequal groups, so as to afford plenty of light to those parts which require it, or bring darkness to bear on other portions which demand such a treatment. The scenic artist, being obliged to put varying tones and shades into his pictures to induce a sense of perspective, is the one, it seems to me, who should be consulted by the person responsible for the stage lighting, in order that the same degrees of light and shade may be preserved. Nothing could be worse than a scene painted in the same tone of colour and in the same shades, there would be neither distance nor perspective ; similarly, if the various portions which make up a complete scene be lighted uniformly, there will be no harmony, no sense of solidity, no contrast and the scene will be ineffective.

Permit me, Sir, to make a digression, which, although foreign to my art, may perhaps be of service to opera.

The dancing warns the machinist to be ready to change the scenery, in fact you know that at the conclusion of the *divertissement* the action passes elsewhere. How is the interval between the acts generally occupied—this interval absolutely necessary for the resetting of the stage, for resting the actors and for the changing of the costumes of the dancers and choruses ? How is the orchestra employed ? In a manner best calculated to destroy all the impression produced on the senses by the act just ended. It plays a *passe-pied*, takes up a *rigaudon* or a still livelier *tambourin*, just when I am moved and affected by the serious events of which I have been a witness, it breaks the charm of a delicious moment, it effaces from my mind the pictures which moved it, it stifles and deadens the feeling in which I took pleasure—nay, this is not all, and you begin to see the length to which stupidity can go ; this emotional drama has only just begun, the next act will see its climax and should reduce me to tears.

Now the orchestra passes from this gay and trivial music to a sad and lugubrious symphony. What a contrast! If the author be once more permitted to restore in me the interest he has made me lose, it will only be very slowly; my thoughts for a long time fluctuate between the distraction he has just made me experience and the sadness it is desired to recall, the illusion, when presented to me a second time, appears too clumsy; I seek to ward it off mechanically in spite of myself, hence the actors must put forth unheard-of efforts in order to enthrall me once more. You must admit that this old method, still so dear to our composers, offends all one's sense of reality. They should not boast of being able to triumph over me to the extent of exciting in my breast, quite suddenly and at their pleasure, all these different emotions. The first act inclines me to surrender myself to the impression produced on me by the objects presented; the interval entirely destroys this first effect, and the result produced on me by the second act is so different and so far removed from my first impression that I can only pick up the thread again with extreme difficulty; especially when my nerves are more inclined to become relaxed in the opposite direction to which they have just been strained. In a word, Sir, this sudden drop, this abrupt passing from the pathetic to the lively, from an enharmonic diatonic or from an enharmonic chromatic to a *gavotte*, or to a kind of *pont-neuf*,[1] seems to me no less discordant than a melody which begins in one key and ends in another. I dare assert that such a discrepancy would always offend those who take pleasure in the emotions afforded by the theatre, for it cannot be perceived by the fribblers who only go there because it is the fashion and who, holding an enormous opera-glass in their hands, prefer the satisfaction of displaying their absurdities, of seeing and being seen, to that of appreciating the pleasure which the united arts can afford them.

Let the poets come down from the sacred Vale, let the artists charged with the different parts which make up an opera work in collaboration and aid each other mutually, and

---

[1] Name given to a popular air. The term has its origin in the fact that, in the seventeenth and early eighteenth centuries, the Paris street vendors of popular songs gathered on the Pont-Neuf to ply their trade. The author wishes to give the impression of a marked contrast.

this type of spectacle will then achieve the greatest success. Talents always succeed when united. It is only a mean-spirited jealousy and wilful misunderstanding, unworthy of fine talents, which wither the arts, degrade those who profess them and hinder the perfection of a work which needs so many details and such varied beauties as opera.

I have always regarded an opera as a fine picture which should express all that painting can offer in the manner of the wonderful and the sublime ; a picture in which the subject should be suggested by the poet and afterwards depicted by painters skilled in the various branches of their art, who, animated solely by honour and a noble ambition to please, should complete the masterpiece in that harmony, that intelligence, which proclaims and characterises true ability. Success depends primarily on the poet, since it is he who places, draws and invests the picture with more or less beauty, more or less action, and consequently more or less interest, according to the measure of his genius. The artists who give expression to his imagination are the composer of the music, the *maître de ballet*, the scenic artist, the costume designer and the machinist ; all five should equally collaborate for the perfection and beauty of the work by following exactly the basic idea of the poet, who, in his turn, must watch carefully over everything. The master's eye is imperative, it must supervise every detail. In opera there is nothing too small or too insignificant ; those things which appear of the least consequence shock, offend and displease when they are not presented with sufficient care and precision. This type of spectacle cannot afford to be mediocre, it captivates in proportion as it is perfect in all its parts. You must agree with me, Sir, that an author who abandons his work to the mercies of five persons whom he never sees, who scarcely know one another, and who take the utmost pains not to come into contact, bears a strong resemblance to those fathers who confide the education of their sons to a stranger, and who, through carelessness or conceit, would think it derogatory to their dignity if they themselves watched over the progress of their offspring. What results from so false a prejudice ? A child born to please becomes bad-tempered and tiresome. Regard the poet as the father, and the dance as the child.

You will tell me, perhaps, that I look upon the poet as a typical man. No, Sir, but a poet must possess wit and taste. I am of the same opinion as the writer who declares that those great works of painting, music and dancing which do not attract the interest of the common herd are bad or mediocre.

Cannot a poet, without being a musician, appreciate whether a certain phrase of music express his thoughts ; whether another do not weaken them ; whether this one lend strength and passion, and give grace and energy to his sentiments ? And, without being a scenic artist, cannot he realise that a scene which is supposed to represent a forest in Africa is more suggestive of that of Fontainebleau, or that which, in another case, should depict an American roadstead resembles rather Toulon ? Again, cannot he realise that the scene which purports to show the palace of some Japanese Emperor is much more related to the palace of Versailles, or lastly, whether the one which should show the gardens of Semiramis resembles those of Marly ?

Without being a dancer or *maître de ballet*, cannot he be similarly aware of the confusion which reigns, or of the lack of expression of the executants ? He can, I say, realise whether the theme be rendered with warmth, whether the groups be sufficiently striking, whether the pantomime be true, whether the spirit of the dance be in accordance with the character of the persons and nations to be represented. Cannot he also be aware of the errors to be encountered in the dresses, due to negligence or bad taste, which, unlike proper theatrical costumes, destroy all illusion ? Does he need to be a machinist to see that a certain device does not act readily ; nothing is more simple than to condemn delay or admire dispatch. Besides, it is the machinist's duty to correct the faulty combination which spoils these effects, their working and their use.

A musical composer must have a knowledge of dancing, or at least be familiar with the time and possibilities of the movements proper to each kind, to each character and to each passion, in order to employ features appropriate to the various situations which the dancer must successively present ; but, so far from taking the pains to acquire the first elements of this art and to learn the theory of it, he avoids the *maître de ballet*, he imagines that it is his art which elevates and gives him superiority over dancing. I shall not dispute with him, although it is only the superiority of a man's art and not the nature of the art which merits such priority and distinction.

The majority of composers follow, I repeat, the time-worn laws of the *Opéra*. They compose *passepieds* because Mlle. Prévost executed them so elegantly ; *musettes* because Mlle. Sallé and M. Dumoulin[1] danced them with both grace and voluptuousness ; *tambourins* because it was the style of dance in which Mlle. Camargo excelled ; and lastly *chaconnes* and *passacailles* because the celebrated Dupré[2] was strongly attached to these movements so adapted to his taste, his style and the nobility of his person ; but all these excellent dancers are dead, they have been succeeded by others ; in some characters they have been surpassed, but in others perhaps they will never be. Mlle. Lany[3] has effaced all those who once shone by virtue of the beauty, precision and boldness of their execution. She is the first dancer in the world ; but we have not forgotten Mlle. Sallé's artless expression ; her graces are always in our thoughts and the affectation of other dancers in her style has not been able to overshadow that nobility and harmonious simplicity of the tender, voluptuous, but always modest movements of that pleasant *danseuse*. No one has yet taken the place of M. Dumoulin ; he danced *pas de deux* with a superiority which it will be difficult to emulate ; always tender, always graceful, sometimes a butterfly, sometimes a breeze, inconstant one moment and faithful the next, always animated by a new

[1] A famous male dancer of the early eighteenth century. P. Rameau, in his *Maître à Danser* (1725), says : " Dumoulin, the last of four most talented brothers, who to-day is still distinguished for his rendering of various characters, was the one who most resembled Ballon, and who consoled the public in some degree for his loss. He also had the advantage of being associated with Mlle. Guiot, an excellent dancer, and by his successful efforts made himself fitted to dance with the illustrious Mlle. Prévost."

[2] Louis Dupré (1697-1774), one of the greatest of French dancers, renowned for the nobility and grace of his movements. He was the teacher of Gaetano Vestris.

[3] Louise Madeleine Lany (1733-1777), a celebrated French dancer, sister of J. B. Lany.

sentiment, he expressed every stage of tender affection with voluptuousness.

M. Vestris[1] has replaced the celebrated Dupré, that is sufficient praise ; but we have M. Lany whose superiority excites one's admiration and raises him above those I might mention, if that would not take me too far from my subject. Lastly, we have legs and a manner of execution which our predecessors never possessed ; this reason should, it seems to me, determine musical composers to be more varied in their works and not to compose only in that manner for which the public recollects a particular style which has almost vanished. The dance of our time is new, it is imperative that the music should be so also.

It is complained that dancers are still stiff in their movements, and, although graceful, are expressionless ; but is it not possible to trace the evil to its source ? Find out the reason for it and you will be able to attack it more advantageously and thus employ remedies necessary to its cure.

I have said that the majority of ballets in this kind of spectacle were cold, although well arranged and well executed ; is it entirely the composer's fault ? Would it be possible for him to think of new ideas every day and to put a *danse d'action* at the end of every act of the opera ? No, undoubtedly, the task would be too difficult to accomplish : besides, such a project cannot be carried out without infinite contradictions, unless poets favour this arrangement and work in collaboration with the *maître de ballet* on all the projects having dancing for their aim.

Let us see what the *maître de ballet* usually does at this spectacle, and let us examine the work he is given to do. He is presented with a prompt copy : he opens it and reads : PROLOGUE : *passepied* for the dancers representing Games and Pleasures ; *gavotte* for the Laughs, and *rigaudon* for the Pleasant Dreams. FIRST ACT : march for the Warriors, second air for the same, *musette* for the Priestesses. SECOND ACT : *loure* for the People, *tambourin* and *rigaudon* for the Sailors. THIRD ACT : march for the Demons, lively air for the same. FOURTH ACT : entry

---

[1] Gaetano Vestris succeeded Dupré as *premier danseur noble* at the Académie Royale de Musique in 1751.

S. L. BOQUET   COSTUME FOR ADONIS (VESTRIS)
From the Bibliothèque de l'Opéra, Paris

of Greeks and *chaconne*, without counting Winds, Tritons, Naiads, Hours, Signs of the Zodiac, Bacchantes, Zephyrs, Shades and Fatal Dreams—because there is no end to them. See how well the *maître de ballet* is instructed ! Witness him entrusted with the execution of a truly magnificent and ingenious plan ! What does the poet demand ? Simply that the members of the ballet dance and are made to dance ; from this abuse are born ridiculous claims.

Sir, says the *premier danseur* to the *maître de ballet*, I take the place of such a dancer and must dance to such an air ; by the same token a certain *danseuse* insists on dancing the *passepieds*, another the *musettes*, this one the *tambourins*, that one the *loures*, and a third the *chaconnes ;* and this imaginary privilege, this dispute about rights and style, supplies each opera with twenty solo *entrées* which are danced in costumes totally opposed in style and manner, but which differ neither in character, atmosphere, combinations of steps nor in the poses ; this monotony has its origin in a mechanical imitation. M. Vestris is the *premier danseur*, he never dances before the last act, that is the rule which conforms to the proverb which reserves the best things till the last. How do the other dancers in this style act ? They distort the original, they caricature it and only reproduce its faults because it is much easier to seize upon mannerisms than to imitate perfections. They follow the example of the courtiers of Alexander the Great who, unable to emulate his valour and heroic virtues, carried their heads on one side to imitate a physical defect of that prince. You continually see miserable plagiarists who represent the original in a hundred different ways and continually disfigure it. Those of another style are no less disagreeable and ridiculous ; they wish to copy the precision, gaiety and beautiful arrangement of M. Lany's *enchaînements*, and they only succeed in making themselves detestable. All the *danseuses* wish to dance like Mlle. Lany, and in this case all of them display ridiculous pretensions.

Finally, Sir, opera is, if I may so express myself, a performance by monkeys. The real man is never seen ; he fears to show himself as he is ; he always borrows from strangers and blushes to be himself ; hence the spectator purchases the pleasure of seeing a few good and original dancers at the cost of the weariness of witnessing a multitude of bad copies which precede them. Moreover, what can be said in favour of that quantity of solo *entrées* which have no relation to the theme ? What signify all these soulless bodies which walk without grace, which move without taste, which pirouette without equilibrium, without stability, and which continue to appear throughout the piece with the same dullness ? Can we accord the title of monologues to these kinds of *entrées* destitute of interest and expression ? Certainly not, because the monologue is part of the action. It is in harmony with the scene ; it paints, relates and instructs. But, you will ask me, how can a solo *entrée* express anything ? Nothing is simpler, Sir, and I will clearly prove it to you.

For instance, two shepherds, smitten with a shepherdess, press her to decide between them : Themira, that is the name of the shepherdess, hesitates, considers, fears to name the victor. Pressed more closely, she gives way to her love and accords the preference to Aristeus ; then flees into the wood to hide her defeat ; but her victor follows her to enjoy his triumph. Tircis, abandoned and scorned, expresses his pain and grief ; soon, jealousy and fury take possession of his heart, he gives way to them and his retreat warns me that he is hastening to take vengeance and slay his rival. An instant later, the latter appears, his every movement conveys to me his extreme happiness ; his gestures, attitudes, facial expression, looks—all reveal to me the picture of sentimental ecstasy. Tircis, in despair, seeks his rival and perceives him at the very moment when he expresses the most delicious and purest joy. There you have two simple but natural contrasts, the happiness of one accentuates the troubles of another. Tircis, in desperation, thinks only of vengeance ; he attacks Aristeus with a fury and impetuosity born of his jealousy and resentment at being despised ; the latter defends himself, but, whether an excess of happiness lowers his courage or whether love requited is the offspring of peace, he is about to succumb to the efforts of Tircis. They use their crooks as weapons, the flowers and garlands lovingly composed for moments of rapture become the trophies of their vengeance. Everything is sacrificed in a moment of fury, and the posy with which Themira had crowned Aristeus does not escape the rage of a lover scorned. However, Themira appears. She perceives her lover bound with the garland she had bestowed on him ; she sees him felled to the ground at the feet of Tircis. What dismay ! What fear ! She shudders at the thought of losing her beloved ; everything expresses her terror, the depth of her passion. What effort she makes to rescue her lover ! Outraged love strengthens her arm. Furious, she seizes an arrow dropped by some huntsman, throws herself on Tircis and strikes him with it several times; at this moving incident the action becomes general, shepherds and shepherdesses hasten from all sides.

Themira, in despair at having commited so base an action, wishes to punish herself by piercing her heart with the arrow, but the shepherds prevent so cruel a design. Aristeus, divided between love and friendship, steals towards Themira and begs and prays her to preserve her life ; he goes to Tircis to render him succour, and asks the shepherds to take care of him. Themira, disarmed, but overcome with sorrow, makes an attempt to approach Tircis. She clasps his knees and affords him ample proofs of a sincere repentance ; he, ever tender, always the passionate lover, seems to cherish the blow which is to end his days. The distracted shepherdesses tear Themira from this spot, the scene of so much misery ; she swoons in their arms. The shepherds on their side carry Tircis away ; he is at the point of death and shows his grief at being parted from Themira and unable to expire in her arms. Aristeus, a firm friend though a faithful lover, expresses his solicitude and anxiety in a hundred different ways. His breast heaves with a thousand combats, he wishes to follow Themira, but is unwilling to forsake Tircis ; he desires to soothe his beloved, but also to comfort his friend. This agitation and cruel indecision comes to an end, an instant's reflection makes friendship triumph over love ; he frees himself from Themira's embraces to fly to the aid of Tircis.

This scenario may appear feeble when read, but will have a splendid effect on the stage, there is not a moment in it which has not interest for a painter ; the many pictures and situations which it offers possess a colouring, an action and an interest ever new. The solo *entrée* of Tircis and that of

Aristeus are full of passion, they depict and express something, therefore they may be accounted true monologues. The two *pas de trois* provide a picture of a dialogue in two different styles, and the *ballet d'action* which concludes this little romance will always have a lively interest for every spectator possessed of a feeling heart and an all-seeing eye, provided that the executants have a soul and a feeling for lively expression.

You will see, Sir, that in order to depict an action full of varied passions and where the changes in them are as sudden as in the scenario I have just outlined, the music must entirely abandon the feeble movements and modulations which are generally employed for dance music. It is not simply a matter of arranging notes according to the rules of a school, the harmonic succession of sounds must in this instance imitate those of nature and suggest the dialogue.

In general, I do not condemn, Sir, the solo *entrées* in an opera. I admire their scattered beauties, but desire less of them. One can have even a surfeit of a good thing. I should like more variety in their execution, because nothing is so ridiculous as to see the shepherds of Tempe dancing like the divinities of Olympus. Dresses and characters being innumerable in such a spectacle I should like the dance not to be always the same. This irritating uniformity would doubtless disappear if the dancers were to study the character of the person they are meant to represent, if they grasped his manners and his ways. It is only by putting themselves in the place of the hero or person to be represented that they can succeed in imitating him perfectly. No one more than I is willing to render greater justice to solo *entrées* danced by the *premiers sujets* when they display all the beauties of the harmonious movements of the body ; but I should like these same illustrious dancers to combine ideas with the graces of their bodies. I should be delighted to admire them in a more seductive form and not to be restricted to look at them only as beautiful machines, well contrived and well proportioned. This would not be to despise their execution, to cheapen their talent and abuse their style ; it is purely to persuade them to embellish and ennoble it.

Let us pass to costume ; its variety and accuracy are as rare as in music, in ballets and in simple dancing. Obstinacy in adhering to out-worn traditions is the same in every part of opera ; it is the monarch of all it surveys. Greek, Roman, Shepherd, Hunter, Warrior, Faun, Forester, Games, Pleasures, Laughs, Tritons, Winds, Fires, Dreams, High Priests, Celebrants—all these characters are cut to the same pattern and differ only in colour and in the ornaments with which a desire for ostentatious display rather than good taste has caused them to be bespattered at caprice. Tinsel glitters everywhere : Peasant, Sailor, Hero—all are covered alike. The more a costume is decorated with gewgaws, spangles, gauze and net, the greater the admiration it procures the player and the ignorant spectator.

At the *Opéra*, few things to be encountered are more curious than the sight of a band of warriors who come to do battle, fight and carry off the victory. Do they bring in their wake all the horrors of carnage ? Are their features aflame ? Are their looks ferocious ? Is their hair dishevelled ? No, Sir, nothing of the kind. They are dressed as if going on parade and resemble effeminate men fresh from a perfumed bath rather than survivors of a desperate struggle. What becomes of truth ? Where is verisimilitude ? How can illusion be suggested ? And how can one fail not to be shocked at so false and ill-conceived a spectacle ? I admit that the bounds of propriety must not be transgressed, but above all the action must display a sense of truth and reality ; the picture must exhibit life and vigour, and an appropriate confusion whenever the theme requires it.

I would do away with those stiff *tonnelets*[1] which in certain dancing positions transport, as it were, the hip to the shoulder and conceal all the contours of the body. I would banish all uniformity of costume, an indifferent, ungraceful device which owes its origin to lack of taste. I should prefer light and simple draperies of contrasting colours, worn in such a manner as to reveal the dancer's figure. I

---

[1] The recognised costume for eighteenth-century dancers in the noble or serious style was the dress of a Roman officer seen through the eyes of eighteenth-century artists. It consisted of a tight-fitting body like the Roman cuirass carried out in material, with sleeves reaching to the waist which were puffed from shoulder to elbow. The base of the body widened out into a short skirt made to assume a hooped shape by being stretched over a light frame. This skirt was called a *tonnelet* (lit. diminution of *tonneau*, a cask).

should like them to be airy, but without stinting the material. I desire beautiful folds, fine masses with the ends fluttering and producing ever-changing forms as the dance becomes more and more animated ; everything should convey a sense of filminess. A bound, a lively step, a taking to flight would waft the drapery in different directions and bring us nearer to a painting and consequently to nature ; that is what affords charm and elegance to poses, and would give to the dancer that sense of briskness which he cannot attain when clad in the mediæval armour ordained by the *Opéra*. I would reduce by three-quarters the ridiculous paniers of our *danseuses*, they are equally opposed to the liberty, speed, prompt and lively action of the dance. Again, they deprive the figure of the elegance and correct proportions which it should have ; they lessen the charms of the arms ; they disguise, as it were, every grace ; they impede and trouble the *danseuse* to such a degree that the movement of her panier generally takes up far more of her attention than that of her arms and legs. Every actor on the stage must be free and unfettered in his movements ; he must not be hindered by the manner of costume necessitated by the character he has to represent. If his thoughts be divided, if the style of a ridiculous costume annoy the dancer so that he feels overcome by the weight of his clothes to the extent of forgetting his part and groans under the burden which overwhelms him, how can he act with ease and warmth ? From that moment he must escape from a fashion which impoverishes his art and hinders all expression. The inimitable actress, Mlle. Clairon,[1] who seemed born to overthrow habits engendered by custom, discarded paniers and suppressed them reckless of the consequences.

Genuine talent knows how to liberate itself from laws of routine. That unerring taste which carried the art of this great actress to so fine a degree of perfection made her realise the absurdity of these old-fashioned theatrical costumes, and, in her endeavour to present a faithful imitation of nature, she rightly came to the conclusion that this

---

[1] Claire Josèphe Hippolyte Leris de La Tude (1723-1803), better known by her assumed name of Clairon, one of the greatest of French tragic actresses. She worked ardently to effect reform in stage costume, contending that all dresses should be historically correct.

S. L. BOQUET   COSTUME FOR PLEASURE (G. VESTRIS)
Note the *tonnelet*
From the Bibliothèque de l'Opéra, Paris

standard must be maintained in matters concerning dress. Mlle. Clairon did not act from caprice when she stripped herself of an ornament as absurd as it was clumsy ; it was because she had studied every branch of her art and sought to bring all of them to perfection. Reason, wit, common sense and nature led her to institute this reform ; she consulted the works of ancient authors and came to the conclusion that Medea, Electra and Ariana would never have had the airs, style, gait and dress of our fine ladies. She felt that in discarding our customs she would approach nearer to those of antiquity ; that the representation of the people she impersonated would be more faithful and more natural ; that her actions would be lively and animated, and that she would render them with more force and energy were she freed of the weight and annoyance of a ridiculous garment. She is now assured that the public will not gauge her talents from the size of her panier.

It is certain that superior talents alone possess the initiative to introduce innovations and to change in a moment those things to which custom rather than taste or reflection have bound us. M. Chassé, an actor of unusual ability who possessed the art of infusing interest into tedious scenes and expressing in gesture the lightest thoughts, similarly discarded *tonnelets* or those stiff paniers which deprived the actor of all freedom and made him resemble, as it were, an ill-contrived machine. Helmets and uniformity of costume were also proscribed by him. He substituted flowing draperies for the stiff *tonnelets*, and plumes arranged with taste and elegance for the old-fashioned tufts of feathers. His attire was simple, manly and picturesque.

The excellent tragedian, M. Lekain,[1] followed M. Chassé's example—he went further. In M. Voltaire's *Semiramis* he came out of the tomb of Ninus with turned-up sleeves, bloody arms, bristling hair and staring eyes. This powerful but natural picture impressed, interested and filled spectators with a sense of calamity and horror. Reflection and a critical sense succeeded the emotion an instant later; but it was too late, the impression was achieved, the actor had gained his point, and rounds of applause were the reward of

[1] Henri Louis Cain, called Lekain (1728-1778), a great French tragedian.

a bold and happy action which would doubtless have miscarried, if an inferior actor had had the temerity to undertake it.

M. Boquet,[1] entrusted with the designing of the costumes for the *Opéra*, has partly remedied the defects which existed in this branch so essential to illusion. It is to be hoped that he will be permitted to continue his work, and that he will not be opposed in those ideas which always tend to bring things to perfection.

As for scenery, Sir, I shall not discuss it ; at the *Opéra* the scenes do not err in the matter of taste, they may even be beautiful, because the artists employed in this branch are really talented. But intrigue and a false sense of economy limit the painters' genius and stifle their talents. Besides at the *Opéra* one is never informed of the names of the artists responsible for the scenes, so that there is little glory to be gained and consequently there are few scenes which do not leave much to be desired.

I shall conclude this letter by what, in my opinion, is a very simple reflection. Dancing in this type of spectacle has too many idyllic characters, too many chimerical persons, too many fantastic beings to portray, for them to be represented with different features and colours. Let us have less of the Fairy Tale, less of the marvellous, more truth and more realism, and dancing will appear to much better advantage. I should be much troubled, for example, to provide a suitable dance for a Comet, the signs of the Zodiac, the Hours, and so on. The interpreters of Sophocles, Euripides, and Aristophanes declare, however, that the dances of the Egyptians represented the movements of heavenly bodies and the harmony of the universe. They dance in a circle around an altar which they regard as the sun, and this figure which they describe holding each other's hands corresponds to the Zodiac, or the circle of signs ; but all this, like many other things, is only a set of conventional movements to which is attached an unvarying significance.

I think then, Sir, it would be easier to depict our fellowmen, that the impersonation of them would be more natural

---

[1] Simon Louis Boquet, an excellent designer of theatrical costumes. Among others, he sketched, under Boucher's direction, the dresses for the opera *Armide*.

S. L. BOQUET   COSTUME FOR BALLET
Note: the attribution to Mlle. Sallé is incorrect
From the Bibliothèque de l'Opéra, Paris

and seductive ; but, as I have said, poets are the men to discover the means of making ordinary mortals appear on the *Opéra* stage. Why should this be impossible ? What has been achieved once can be successfully repeated a thousand times. It is certain that the tears of Andromache, the love of Junia and Britannicus, the passion of Merope for Ægisthus, the submission of Iphigenia and the eternal love of Clytemnestra would be much more interesting than our present Fairy Tales. Blue Beard and Riquet with the Tuft appeal to children only ; feelings common to humanity are the only ones which touch, move and transport the soul. Fabulous divinities are of little interest, because it is felt that their power and intelligence are due to the poet alone. There is never any doubt about their success, and that they will achieve their aim ; their power diminishes in proportion as our confidence increases. The heart and mind are never deceived by this spectacle. It is rare, not to say impossible, for a spectator to leave the *Opéra* with that emotion and delightful feeling which he experiences after an affecting tragedy or comedy. The state into which they throw us would continue for a long while, if the pleasing pictures of our little trifles did not calm our feelings and dry our tears.

I am, &c.

LETTER IX

AS you know, Sir, a man's face is the mirror of his passions, in which the movements and agitations of the soul are displayed, and in which tranquillity, joy, sadness, fear and hope are expressed in turn. This expression is a hundred times more animated, more lively and more precious than that which results from the most impassioned harangue. If one be deprived of the sight of the facial expression of the orator, it requires a little time to fathom his meaning. It requires no time for the face to express its meaning forcibly; a flash of lightning comes from the heart, shines in the eyes and, illumining every feature, heralds the conflicts of passions, and reveals, so to speak, the naked soul. All our movements are purely automatic and meaningless, if the face remain speechless and do not animate and invigorate them.

Physiognomy then is that part of us most necessary to expression; well, why conceal it on the stage by a mask, and prefer a clumsy art to beautiful nature? How can the dancer paint if he be deprived of his most essential colours? How can he transfer to the breast of the spectator the passions that consume his own, if he himself remove the means and cover his face with a piece of cardboard which ever appears sad and uniform, cold and motionless? The face is the vehicle of the mimic scene, the faithful interpreter of all the movements in pantomime; there you have ample reason for banishing masks from dancing, that imitative art in which every action must seek to delineate, captivate and move by the artlessness and truth of its pictures.

I should be greatly troubled to fathom a painter's intention and to conceive the subject he wished to transfer to canvas, if all the heads of the figures were as alike as those of the dancers at the *Opéra*, and if their features and characteristics

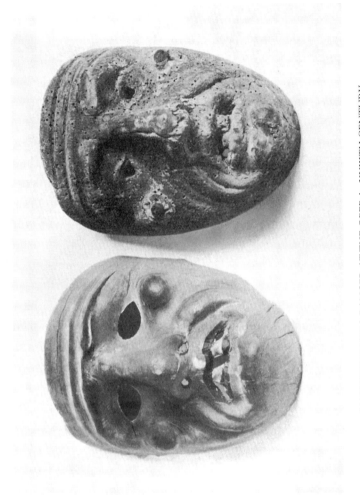

MASK WORN BY A DANCER AT THE OPERA, XVIIITH CENTURY

The mask is made of leather and presumably represents a Rustic. The original mould is also shown

From the Musée de l'Opéra, Paris

were not varied. I could not understand, I say, what prompts one person to raise his arm, and another to have his hand on his sword-hilt; it would be impossible for me to understand the emotion which makes this one raise his head and arms, and that one retreat. If all the figures were drawn according to the rules of art and in the likeness of nature, it would be hard for me to grasp the artist's intention; I should consult each face in vain. They would be dumb, their monotonous features would tell me nothing, their dull, vacuous expressions would be meaningless; I could not refrain from regarding this picture as a very imperfect copy of nature, because I should not encounter the variety which embellishes it and makes it ever new.

Will the public more easily perceive a dancer's thoughts and intention, if he unceasingly conceal his features beneath a foreign body, if he veil his thoughts and substitute for his natural features those of an ill-designed plaster cast painted in the most disagreeable manner? Can the passions be revealed and break through the screen which the dancer places between the spectator and himself? Can he make a single one of those artificial faces express the innumerable characteristics of the different passions? Will it be possible for him to change the form which the mould has given to the mask? Because the mask of whatever kind is either cold or pleasing, serious or comic, sad or grotesque. The modeller affords it but one permanent and unvarying character.

If he easily succeed in making hideous and deformed faces, and those which are purely imaginary, he has not the same success when he forsakes his caricatures and tries to imitate beautiful nature. If he stop making grimaces he becomes dull, his moulds are devoid of expression, his masks are characterless and lifeless; he cannot reproduce the subtleties of the features and all the imperceptible shades which grouping themselves, so to speak, on the face, accord it a thousand different forms; what modeller can undertake to render the passions in all their infinite gradations? Can that immense variety which sometimes eludes the cleverest painter and which is the touchstone of the great master be sold by a maker of masks? No, Sir, Ducreux' shop was never that of nature, his masks were only a caricature of nature and resembled it not at all.

It would be necessary, in order to permit the use of masks in the *danse d'action*, to put as many kinds on the face as Don Japhet of Armenia put skull-caps of different colours on his head, to don and doff them in succession according to the circumstances and corresponding movements which are gone through in a *pas de deux*. But it is the custom to adopt an easier practice, to retain an artificial face which expresses nothing, and the dance which resembles it speaks no better ; it is totally inanimate.

Those who like masks and are habitually accustomed to them, and who believe that the art would degenerate if the yoke of the ancient laws of the *Opéra* were thrown off, declare, to excuse their bad taste, that there are theatrical characters which require masks, such as Fairies, Tritons, Winds, Fauns and so forth. This argument is ridiculous ; it is based on a prejudice as easy to oppose as to vanquish. First, I shall prove that the masks used for these kinds of characters are ill-modelled, badly painted, and possess no sort of resemblance whatsoever ; secondly, that it is easy to render these personages faithfully and without outside help. Next, I shall support my assertions by living examples which cannot be refuted if one be a child of nature, if simplicity captivate you, if truth be preferable to that exaggerated art which destroys illusion and weakens the spectator's pleasure.

The characters which I am about to cite to you are purely imaginary ; they have been created by poets ; painters have given them an air of reality by endowing them with different features and attributes, which are varied in proportion as the arts have become perfected and as the torch of taste has lighted the way for artists. Winds are no longer painted nor danced with whistles in the hand, windmills on the head and feathered costumes to express their airiness. The World is no longer painted or danced with a head-dress which would rival Mount Olympus, and a costume representing a geographical map ; the dress is no longer covered with inscriptions, nor does one write on the breast or the left side, GALLIA ; on the stomach, GERMANIA ; on one leg, ITALIA ; on the posteriors, TERRA AUSTRALIS INCOGNITA ; on one arm, HISPANIA ; and so on.

Music is no longer suggested by a costume scored with many staves and covered with crotchets and demi-semi-

quavers, the hair is no longer dressed with the clefs of
G-re-sol, C-sol-ut and *F-ut-fa*. A dancer taking the part of
a Lie no longer appears with a wooden leg, a dress decorated
with masks, and a dark lantern in his hand; these crude
allegories are out of date, but, being unable to consult nature
in regard to chimerical beings, let us at least consult painters.
They represent Winds, Furies and Demons in human form;
Fauns and Tritons have the upper part of the body in the
likeness of man and the lower in the form of a goat and fish
respectively. Tritons' masks are green and silver; those
of Demons red and silver; those of Fauns a blackish-brown;
those of Winds have distended cheeks as in blowing: such
are our masks. Let us see now in comparing them with
masterpieces of painting whether they bear any resemblance
to them.

I see in the most valuable paintings some Tritons whose
physiognomies are not green in the least. I perceive Fauns
and Satyrs of a reddish and bronzed tint, but a sombre brown
is not uniformly distributed over all their features; I look
for faces coloured red and silver, but in vain. The Demons
have a reddish tint which borrows its colour from the element they inhabit. All this is natural for I see it on all sides.
It is never lost under the thickness of the paint or the weight
of a big brush; I recognise in them the form of every
feature. They may be hideous and caricatured, if you will,
but everything reveals the man to me, not as he is, but as
he can be without offending verisimilitude. Besides, should
not man necessarily differ from those fictitious beings born
in the poet's brain, and must not elemental beings differ in
some way from man ? The masks of the Winds are those
which most resemble the originals which painters have
given us, and if a mask be needed on the stage, this is surely
the one. Two reasons make me think so; first, the difficulty of retaining this puffed-out face for any length of time;
secondly, the little possibility of expression in this type.
The Wind says nothing, it turns with rapidity, it has a great
deal of movement and little action. It is a whirlwind of
steps without taste and often dazzles without satisfying,
surprises without interesting, and thus the mask conceals
nothing. This type, Sir, I find so dull and so tedious that
I would even agree to the dancer's wearing several of them,

if by this means he thought himself able to interest those who admire masks. With the exception of Boreas in the ingenious ballet *Les Fleurs*, no Winds at the *Opéra* have seemed to me other than tedious and out of place.

Would it not be possible by abolishing masks to induce dancers to make up their faces in a more picturesque and more realistic manner ? Can they not replace the shades caused by distance, with the aid of some artistically placed light colours, and, by means of lines painted with a brush, give to their faces the particular character they should possess ? This proposal cannot be set aside without ignoring what nature can produce when it is aided and embellished by the charms of art ; it cannot be condemned except by totally ignoring the seductive effect which results from this arrangement and the interesting changes which it carries out without disfiguring nature, without weakening her features, without caricaturing her. One example will support this truth, it will afford it the power to persuade men of taste and convince a crowd of incredulous fools with which the stage is overwhelmed.

Mr. Garrick, the celebrated English actor, is the model I wish to put forward. Not only is he the most handsome, the most perfect and the most worthy of admiration of all actors, he may be regarded as the Proteus of our own time ; because he understood all styles and presented them with a perfection and truth which aroused not only the applause and praise of his countrymen, but also excited the admiration and encomiums of all foreigners. He was so natural, his expression was so lifelike, his gestures, features and glances were so eloquent and so convincing, that he made the action clear even to those who did not understand a word of English. It was easy to follow his meaning ; his pathos was touching ; in tragedy he terrified with the successive movements with which he represented the most violent passions. And, if I may so express myself, he lacerated the spectator's feelings, tore his heart, pierced his soul, and made him shed tears of blood.

In comedy he captivated and enchanted ; he was diverting in farce ; while his make-up on the stage was so artistically contrived that frequently he passed unrecognised by those who habitually lived with him. You are familiar with the

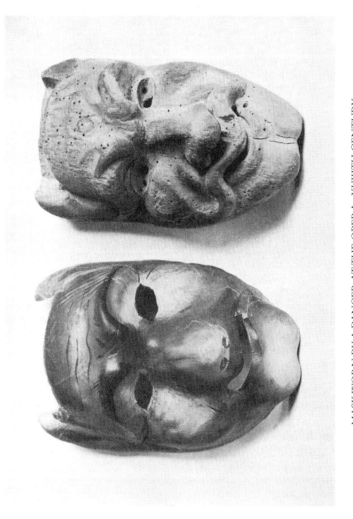

MASK WORN BY A DANCER AT THE OPERA, XVIIITH CENTURY

The mask is made of leather and represents a Faun. The original mould is also shown

From the Musée de l'Opéra, Paris

immense number of characters in the English drama ; he played them all with the same mastery ; he had, as it were, a different face for each part. He knew how to dispose brush strokes on the prominent parts of the face according to the needs of the character he was playing ; he selected his colours and brushes according to the age, condition, character, calling and rank of the person to be represented. Do not think that this great actor was common, trivial and a caricaturist; a faithful worshipper of nature, he knew the value of selection, he preserved that sense of propriety which the stage requires even in the parts least susceptible of grace and charm. He never over-acted or under-acted a character which he represented ; he gave just that exact interpretation which other actors nearly always miss ; that happy sense of proportion which characterises the great actor and which leads to truth is a rare talent which Mr. Garrick possessed—a talent all the more estimable since it prevents the actor going astray and deceiving himself in the colours he employs in his pictures. For coldness is often mistaken for modesty, monotony for reason, stiffness for a noble presence, affectation for grace, shouting for passion, a multiplicity of gestures for action, idiotic conduct for artlessness, volubility in one key for eloquence, and facial contortions for lively expression of the soul.

This was never the case with Mr. Garrick ; he studied the characters of his personages, and still more their passions. Strongly attached to his profession, he shut himself up and would see no one on the days he played important parts. His genius raised him to the rank of the prince he must portray, he assumed all his virtues and frailties, he assimilated the character and its foibles, and was a man transformed. It was no longer Garrick to whom one spoke ; it was no longer Garrick whom one heard ; the change once effected, the actor disappeared and the hero was revealed; and the actor did not become his natural self until his task was done.

You imagine, Sir, that he was rarely at liberty, that his being was always agitated, that his imagination laboured unceasingly, that three parts of his life were spent in an exhausting enthusiasm which affected his health in proportion as he worried himself to evoke a condition resulting

from some sad and unfortunate incident—twenty hours before depicting and delivering it.

Yet who could be more gay when on the contrary he was to play the part of a poet, a workman, a man of the people, a short-story-writer or a dandy ; because this type of person exists in England too, although it is true in a different manner than in our country. The species differ, if you will, but the expression of ridicule and impertinence is the same. In these kinds of characters his features changed artlessly, he always acted with his mind, at each moment his features revealed new thoughts depicted with great truth. He could, quite impartially, be considered as the English Roscius, because to diction, delivery, fire, native wit and delicacy he united that rare gift for pantomimic expression which characterises the great actor and perfect comedian.

I shall add only one word more regarding this distinguished actor to prove the superiority of his talents. I have seen him represent a tragedy which he had touched up, because in addition to his merits as an actor he was one of the most pleasing poets of his country. I have seen him represent a tyrant who, appalled at the enormity of his crime, dies torn with remorse. The last act was given up to regrets and grief, humanity triumphed over murder and barbarism ; the tyrant, obedient to the voice of conscience, denounced his crimes aloud ; they gradually became his judges and his executioners ; the approach of death showed each instant on his face ; his eyes became dim, his voice could not support the efforts he made to speak his thoughts. His gestures, without losing their expression, revealed the approach of his last moment ; his legs gave way under him, his face lengthened, his pale and livid features bore the signs of suffering and repentance. At last, he fell ; at that moment his crimes peopled his thoughts with the most horrible forms ; terrified at the hideous pictures which his past acts revealed to him, he struggled against death ; nature seemed to make one supreme effort. His plight made the audience shudder, he clawed the ground and seemed to be digging his own grave, but the dread moment was nigh, one saw death in reality, everything expressed that instant which makes all equal. In the end he expired. The death-rattle and the convulsive movements of the features, arms and breast, gave the final touch to this terrible picture.

That is what I have seen, Sir, and that is what actors should see. In imitating this great artist it would not be difficult to abolish masks because then the features would be expressive and animated, and would possess the ability to characterise the emotions with as much wit and art as Garrick himself.

Many persons assert that masks serve two purposes : first, to give uniformity ; secondly, to hide the nervous starts and grimaces produced by the efforts called for by a difficult feat of technique. It is a question whether this uniformity be a blessing ; for myself, I regard it quite differently, I find that it falsifies truth and destroys verisimilitude. Is nature uniform in her productions ? In what nation on earth is everyone alike ? Is not everything different ? Has not everything in the universe a different shape and colour ? Does a tree put forth two exactly similar leaves, or flowers, or fruits ? Undoubtedly the variations of nature's productions are infinite ; their variety is immense and incomprehensible. If you rarely find two men alike, if the resemblance in features and form of two twins be admired as a *lusus naturæ*, what would be my surprise if I saw at the *Opéra* twelve faces exactly alike ! And what would be my astonishment if I found one face common to the Greeks, Romans, Shepherds, Sailors, Games, Laughs, Pleasures, and Priests ! How absurd it would be, especially in a piece where all is varied, all is in movement, where scenes change and nations follow one another, where the costumes differ at each moment while the faces of the dancers are always the same. Where there is no diversity of expression in the features, everything languishes and nature groans under a deathly and disagreeable mask.

Why should we permit actors and choristers to retain their natural features, while we rob those who need them more than they, since they are deprived of speech ? How absurd it is that Pan and half the Fauns and Dryads of his band should have white faces while the other half wear brown masks. The Demons who dance are fire-coloured, and those by their side are of a pale and livid tint. Sea Gods, Tritons, River Gods, Water Sprites—all are unmasked when they sing. But when they dance, their faces are grass-green, and they would hardly be noticed at a masquerade where fancy dress was compulsory. So this pretence of uniformity is absolutely destroyed. Is it necessary that everyone should be masked? What would happen if masks were abolished, since the very reasons which prohibit their use by players are the same which should proscribe their use by dancers? You observe, Sir, that all fantastic faces are only devised to shock those who are lovers of the True, the Simple and the Natural.

But let us consider the question of nervous habits, a subject so slight as to appear hardly worthy of discussion. Nervous starts, convulsions and grimaces are less the result of habit than that of the violent efforts made when jumping —efforts which contracting all the muscles make the features grimace in a hundred different ways, and by these signs I perceive only a galley-slave, and not a dancer and an artist. Every dancer whose face alters as the result of his physical efforts, and whose features are continually in a state of convulsion, is a bad dancer who disregards the first principles of his art, who concerns himself only with the mechanical side of dancing, and who has never penetrated its spirit. Such a person is only fitted to attempt dangerous leaps; the spring-board should be his stage since he sacrifices the miming, spirit and charm of his art to a debasing routine, for, instead of studying how to depict and feel, he applies himself only to the physical side of his talent. Lastly, since his physiognomy displays only anxiety and strain when, on the contrary, it should show nothing but ease and freedom, such a man is only a blunderer whose painful execution is always disagreeable.

What is more pleasing to us than grace born of facility? Difficulties have no right to please except when they are unrealised and borrow that noble and easy appearance which, concealing the labour, displays only ease. The *danseuses* of our time have a proportionately greater facility of performance than men; they do everything that it is possible to do. I will ask therefore why *danseuses* maintain a graceful facial expression during their most violent movements? Why do not the facial muscles contract when the human machine is shaken by a succession of violent shocks? Why

MASK WORN BY A DANCER AT THE OPERA, XVIIITH CENTURY

The mask is made of leather and represents an Old Man. The original mould is also shown

From the Musée de l'Opéra, Paris

have women, who are naturally less sinewy, less muscular and less strong than we, have tender and voluptuous, lively and animated expressions, even when their muscles which co-operate in their movements are in a condition of unnatural strain ? How, then, do they acquire that art which conceals labour, which hides bodily stress, and substitutes the most delicate and tender expressions for the grimaces born of the exertions put forth ? The reason is that they pay particular attention to their exercises ; they realise that a contortion disfigures the beauty of the face and changes its expression. They realise that the face is, as I have said, that part of us in which all expression is concentrated, and which is the faithful mirror of our feelings, movements and affections. Hence they put more soul, more expression and more interest into their work than men. And if the latter took the same pains as the women, they would be neither hideous nor displeasing, nor contract vicious habits any longer ; they would have no more nervous mannerisms and could dispense with a mask which in this instance aggravates the evil without destroying it. It is a plaster which conceals imperfections from our eyes to show others still more disagreeable. There is no remedy if the face be continually hidden. In fact, what advice can be given to a mask ? However good the counsel, the mask would be always cold and lifeless.

Strip the physiognomy of this foreign body, abolish this custom which conceals the play of the soul and prevents its expression in the features, then one will be able to judge the dancer and gauge his power of expression. The one who brings a lively and animated sense of pantomime and rare appreciation of feeling to the difficulties and graces of the art will receive the title of excellent dancer and good actor ; praise will encourage him, the advice and counsels of connoisseurs will guide him to perfection in his art. Then he will be told : " Your face was too cold in that scene ; in another place, your looks were not animated enough ; the sentiment which you had to depict not being sufficiently realised by you in your heart was not expressed outwardly with sufficient force and energy, so your gestures and attitudes betrayed the little fire which you put into your action. Another time give full rein to your imagination, probe the spirit of the scene which you have to represent and never forget that to express properly one must not only feel, but feel with all one's heart." Such advice, Sir, would make dancing in as flourishing a condition as pantomime was in the time of the ancients, and would accord it a distinction that it never will attain so long as routine prevails over good taste.

You must allow me to state my preference for lively and animated features. Variety of expression distinguishes people from one another; it indicates what we are and obviates that general confusion which would reign in the universe, if we all resembled each other as much as the dancers at the *Opéra*.

You have told me many times that in order to abolish masks every dancer should have a face suitable for the stage. I am entirely of this opinion, and I have no use for a sad and expressionless visage like that of a mask, but, as there are three styles of dancing according to the height, and different types of faces, so dancers, by a careful and just self-examination, could employ their particular qualities to the best advantage. They all have the same object in whatever style they adopt; they must imitate and mime, it is simply a question of making dancing express a more or less elevated language according to the dignity of the theme and the style of the piece.

The serious and heroic style itself bears the impression of tragedy; the semi-serious, generally known as *demi-caractère*, bears the impression of high comedy; whereas the grotesque dance borrows its features from low and broad comedy. The historical pictures of the celebrated Vanloo are typical of the serious dance, those of the gallant and inimitable Boucher represent those of *demi-caractère*, and, finally, those of the incomparable Teniers resemble the comic dance. The genius of the three dancers who take up these particular styles should be as different as their heights, their features, and their type of mind. The first should be tall, the second gallant, and the last comic. The first will draw his themes from history and mythology, the second from pastorals, and the third from boorish and rustic sources. And if there exist any man who cannot give a character to his face, he should leave the stage for ever.

It is no less important that these three kinds of dancers should have wit, taste and imagination like the three great painters in their different styles. They should seize upon that moment of truth and that correct imitation which makes the copy worthy to rank with the original, and shows the real object in the one imitated.

A dancer in the serious style undoubtedly requires a noble and elegant stature. Those who devote themselves to this style have the most difficulties to surmount and the most obstacles to overcome in order to attain perfection. It is difficult for such a one to make a favourable impression. The longer his limbs, the more difficult it is for him to make them rounded, to move them gracefully. Everything in little children is seductive and charming ; their gestures and attitudes are full of grace ; their contours are admirable. If this charm diminish, if such a child cease to please, if his arms appear less shapely and his head has no longer that charm which captivates the spectator, it is because he has begun to grow, so that his limbs being longer lose their prettiness, since beauties brought together in a small compass appear to greater advantage than when they are scattered. The eye likes to see beauties, but not to seek for them.

A dancer in the *demi-caractère* and voluptuous style undoubtedly requires to be of a medium height which can partake of all the beauties of elegant stature. Of what importance is height, if an agreeable proportion reign over all parts of the body and accord it that grace and artless expression to be seen in the countryside ?

A dancer in the comic style needs fewer physical perfections ; the shorter he be, the more will his body afford grace and attractive charm to his expression.

As their heights differ so must their faces. A noble air, fine features, a proud bearing, a majestic look—that is the mask of the dancer in the serious style.

Less fine features, an agreeable and attractive bearing, a face suitable for the expression of tenderness and voluptuousness—that is the physiognomy required by the dancer in the *demi-caractère* and pastoral style.

Pleasant features, alive with good humour and high spirits, are the only ones suitable for dancers in the comic style. They should reflect simplicity and natural good humour.

It is not a question, Sir, of dispensing with a mask in order to succeed, but of studying oneself. Let us consult our mirror often, it is a fine teacher which will always reveal our faults and indicate to us the means of mitigating and eradicating them, if we go before it free from self-esteem and ridiculous prejudices. The nature of beauty is of much less importance to the features than that of wit. All those features which, without being regular, are animated by sentiment, please far more than those which, in spite of their beauty, are devoid of expression and vivacity. Again, the stage is a help to the actor, the artificial light generally emphasises the features, and those which are intelligent always gain through being seen on it. Besides, Sir, dancers who are deficient in their statures, features and intelligence, and who have obvious and repulsive defects, should renounce the stage and take up, as I have said already, another occupation which demands less bodily and facial perfection. On the other hand, all those who are favoured by nature, who have a lively and pronounced predilection for dancing, and who, as it were, are called to the service of that art, should learn to adapt and devote themselves to the style of dancing to which they are truly suited. If care be not exercised there can be no success, no superiority. Molière would never have triumphed if he had tried to be a Corneille or a Racine—there never would have been a Molière.

If Préville[1] has not impersonated royalty, it is because his agreeable and good-natured features would have aroused laughter rather than awe ; and if he excel in his profession it is because he has known how to choose the style best suited to him and for which he was born. Lany, for the same reason, has devoted himself to the comic style, because this style seemed made for him, or rather because he seemed made for this style ; he would have been superseded and never have risen, if he had essayed to adopt the style favoured by the celebrated Dupré.

Finally, M. Sarrazin would never have played buffoon parts and other characters of low comedy. The nobility

[1] Pierre Louis Dubas, called Préville (1721-1799), a celebrated French comedian.

of his soul, the majesty of his appearance, his features so well adapted to express pathos and to force from us the tear of sympathy would have been unsuited to low characters that require as little talent as physical perfection. M. Vestris, in his turn, forsook the burlesque style of dancing in order to devote himself to the noble and serious style, a manner of dancing of which he has been the most perfect model.

To raise dancing to that degree of the sublime which it lacks and yet might so easily attain, dancing-masters should follow in their lessons the same course as painters observe in those which they give to their pupils. They begin by making them draw an oval, they next pass to the different parts of the face and then combine them to make a head ; so with the other parts of the body. When the pupil has arrived at that stage when he can put together a whole figure, the master teaches him to recognise natural movements, shows him how to arrange with art those pencil strokes which bestow life and imprint on the features the passions and affections with which the soul is affected.

The dancing-master, like the painter, after having taught his pupil certain steps, the manner of combining one with the other, the opposition of the arms, the *effacements* of the body and the positions of the head, must still show him how to give value and expression to them by the help of the features. In order that he may succeed, it will only be necessary to arrange *entrées* for him in which he would have many passions to represent. It would not be sufficient to make him depict these same passions in all their force, it would still be necessary for him to be taught the succession of their movements, their degrees of light and shade, and the different effects which they produce on the features. From such lessons, dancing would learn to speak, and the dancer to reason ; he would learn to depict while learning to dance and accord a merit to our art which would make it much more appreciated.

But in the present state of affairs a good painting moves one far more than a ballet. In the former I observe plan, reason, and precision in the whole ; accuracy of costume, fidelity to historical truth, life in the faces, striking and varied characters in the heads, and expression everywhere ;

it is nature presented to us by the skilful hands of art ; but in the latter I see nothing but pictures as defective in composition as they are badly drawn. Here is my opinion, and if the path I am about to trace were followed exactly, masks would be broken and the idol trampled under foot to devote oneself to nature, when the dance will produce effects so striking that one will be obliged to place it on a level with painting and poetry.

If our *maîtres de ballet* were ingenious authors, if our dancers were excellent actors, where would be the difficulty of dividing dancing into its parts, and of following the custom that comedy has imposed upon it ? Ballets being poems, they, like dramatic works, demand a certain number of persons for their representation, hence one would no longer say that one dancer excels in the *chaconne*,[1] another shines in the *loure ;*[2] one *danseuse* is admirable in *tambourins*,[3] another unique in *passepieds*,[4] and a third superior in *musettes*.[5] But one would declare then (and this praise would be much more flattering) that one dancer is inimitable in tender and voluptuous characters, another is excellent in tyrannical parts, and in all which require a strong action : one *danseuse* is captivating in the character of a lover, another is incomparable in the representation of fury, while a third renders spiteful scenes with singular fidelity.

I understand that such an arrangement could not happen if the composers limited themselves to a single style, and if dancers did not forsake that passion for mechanically moving their legs and arms.

[1] A moderately slow dance in 3-4 time. Lully made the *chaconne* the usual ending to his operas. The name is derived from the Spanish *chacona*, which in turn is said to have come from the Basque *chocune*, meaning pretty.

[2] A dance slower than a *gigue* and generally in 6-4 time. The name is derived from the *loure*, a kind of bag-pipe, common to many parts of France, especially Normandy, which provided the accompaniment.

[3] An old *Provençal* dance, generally in 2-4 time, which was performed to the flute and tambour de Basque. When the dance was transferred to the theatre the drum accompaniment remained a characteristic feature.

[4] A dance said to have been originated by the sailors of *Basse-Bretagne*. In character it resembled a *menuet* given with a quick step.

[5] A pastoral dance, smooth and simple in character, and generally in 2-4, 3-4, or 6-8 time. The name is derived from the *musette*, a kind of bag-pipe.

Such is the character of fine dancing that reason must be substituted for imbecility, wit for *tours de force*, expression for difficulties, pictures for *cabrioles*, graces for affectation, feeling for mechanical movements of the feet, and the varied character of the human face for those lifeless masks which lead nowhere.

It might still be urged against me that a mask in the serious style bears the character of nobility and does not conceal the dancer's eyes, so that in their glances can be read the passions which affect them. I shall reply: first, that a face which has one expression only is not a face for the stage ; secondly, that a mask having thickness and being the result of a mould, the form of which differs from the face it is to conceal, it is impossible for it to fit the features exactly ; not only does it make the head larger and cause it to lose its proper proportions, but it buries and stifles the looks. Supposing even that it did not deprive the eyes of the expression they should have, would it not be opposed to the alteration which passions produce in the lines and colour of the features ? Can the public see these passions arise, perceive their development and follow the dancer in all his movements ? Are the eyes the sole indication of feeling ?

Defenders of masks will argue that the imagination will supply that which is hidden from us, and when we see the eyes gleaming with jealousy we must think we see the rest of the features glowing with the fire of that passion. No, Sir, the imagination, however lively it may be, cannot lend itself to nonsense of that kind. Eyes expressing tenderness when the features depict hate ? Looks full of fury while the features are gay and jovial ? Those are contrasts which are never encountered in nature and which are too revolting for the imagination, however complacent it may be, to be able to conciliate them. That, then, is the effect produced by a serious mask ; always graceful, it cannot change its character, while the eyes alter at every moment.

Apologists for the mask will say that counterfeit faces have been in use for more than two thousand years, but that means simply that in this respect we have been at fault for two thousand years; this error pardonable among the ancients, cannot be considered so by the moderns.

Formerly, performances were as much for the people

as for those of a certain position. Everyone was admitted, rich and poor alike ; it was necessary to have vast enclosures to hold an infinite number of spectators, who would have failed to find the pleasure they sought, if recourse had not been made to enormous masks, a paunch, false calves, and buskins with very high heels.

But, nowadays, our theatres are smaller with a considerably lesser capacity, and the door is shut against the person who does not pay, hence there is no need to supplement the effect of distance. Actors and dancers must appear on the stage in their natural proportions, the mask becomes foreign to them, it only conceals the thoughts in their minds, and is an obstacle to the progress and perfection of their art.

However, it will still be said that masks were invented for the dance. What does that prove ? But there is no certainty regarding this, Sir ; it would appear that they were invented for use in tragedy and comedy. In order that we may be sure on this point, and to convince ourselves, let us go back to their origin.

According to Quintilian,[1] Orpheus[2] and Linus[3] mentioned them in their poems ; but what was their use in the theatre at that time ? They were not yet known.

> Thespis who came after them,
> . . . was the first who, daubed with lees of wine,
> conducted through the towns this happy band,
> and, filling a cart with ill-clad actors,
> amused the passers-by with a new spectacle.

> Æschylus succeeded him and
> . . . used actors in choruses whose faces he
> covered with more honest masks and caused the
> actors to appear, shod in buskins, on the planks
> of a stage erected before the public.

[1] M. Fabius Quintilianus (A.D. 40—A.D. 118), a celebrated Roman rhetorician.

[2] A mythological personage in Greek legend, the chief representative of the art of song and playing on the lyre, and the most illustrious poet of the pre-Homeric period.

[3] A figure of Greek legend ; the personification of a dirge or lamentation.

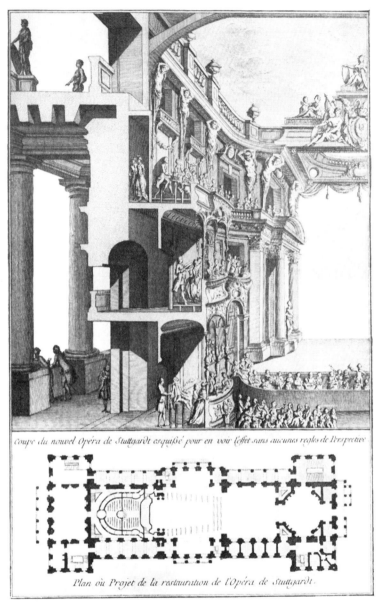

Coupe du nouvel Opéra de Stuttgardt esquissé pour en voir l'effet sans aucunes regles de Perspective

Plan où Projet de la restauration de l'Opéra de Stuttgardt.

VERTICAL SECTION OF AN XVIIITH CENTURY THEATRE
From Diderot & D'Alembert's "Encyclopédie," 1751-72

Here is a mention of masks, but were they made for dancers ? The authors explain nothing and speak of actors only.

Sophocles and Euripides, who came later, introduced nothing new ; they only perfected tragedy and changed the masks of Æschylus to accord with the different characters of their pieces.

A little later in the same period came Crates,[1] who wrote in the manner of the Sicilian poets Epicharmus[2] and Phormis ;[3] he gave to comedy plays which were better constructed and less free. History relates nothing of what they achieved for masks ; perhaps they devised some means to differentiate the comic from the tragic masks.

I consult Aristophanes and Menander,[4] but they tell me nothing. I notice that the former, in his piece called *The Clouds*, presents Socrates on the stage and makes this character wear a mask which, since it excited the derision of the populace, doubtless caricatured that great philosopher's features.

I pass to the Romans : Plautus and Terence make no mention of masks used in pantomimes. I see in ancient manuscripts, on intaglios, on medals and the *en têtes* to Terence's Comedies, masks quite as hideous as those used at Athens.

Roscius and Æsop fascinate me, but these are actors and not dancers. I strive in vain to discover the period when masks originated at Rome—a useless quest. Diomedes says well that it was a Roscius Gallus who was the first to use them in order to conceal a defect in his eyes, but he does not inform me when Roscius lived ; that which was originally used to hide a physical defect at once became necessary having regard to the immensity of the theatres, and enormous masks were made, as at Athens. Big eyes set aslant, large and gaping mouth, hanging lips, pimples on the forehead, distended cheeks—such were the masks of the ancients.

[1] Crates of Athens, a comic poet who flourished about B.C. 449.

[2] The chief comic poet among the Dorians, *b.* B.C. 540, *d.* B.C. 450.

[3] One of the originators of Comedy, who flourished about B.C. 478.

[4] Menander of Athens (B.C. 342—B.C. 292), the most distinguished poet of the New Comedy.

To these masks was added a kind of horn or speaking trumpet, which carried sounds clearly to the most distant spectators ; these trumpets were lined with brass. There was also employed a kind of marble, which Pliny calls *calcophonus*, or brass-sound, because it gave a sound similar to this metal.

The ancients had also masks with two faces ; the profile on the right side was gay, that on the left was sad and ill-tempered. The actor took care, according to the exigencies of the case and situation in which he found himself, to present that side of the mask which was analogous to the action which he had to represent.

Lastly, critical masks were made ; citizens were accorded the right to act, and the sculptors charged with the manufacture of the masks copied those used in the public performances.

These enormous masks were carved out of wood and were a considerable weight ; they completely enveloped the head and rested on the shoulders, which acted as a base. I leave you to consider, Sir, if it be possible to imagine that such burdens were created for the dance, and then add the trappings, the paunch, calves, false thighs and stilts, and you will see that it is improbable that this accoutrement could have been invented for an art which is the child of freedom, which fears the shackles of an embarrassing fashion, and which ceases to appear the moment it ceases to be free.

This costume was so burdensome and inconvenient that the actor made no movement when reciting. The declamation was divided between two persons, one made the gestures while the other spoke.

One is almost tempted to believe that dancing, as understood by the ancients, was entirely different from that of our days, because how can we reconcile our lively and brilliant manner of execution with the heavy trappings worn by the Greeks and the Romans ?

It is true, said Lucian, that the masks used in pantomime were not as exaggerated as those worn by actors, that this equipment was suitable and convenient; but were the masks any smaller ? Did dancers possess the means to inflate and magnify themselves ? Were they better able to manage the diminishing effect of distance than the actors ? It would be absurd to think so. These, then, would have appeared giants and the others pygmies.

There you have, Sir, the only passage which can lead us to think that the mimes used masks ; but neither in ancient authors, nor in modern writers who have treated of the matter, is there anything which can convince me that these colossal faces would have been dwarfed for the purpose of the dance.

Lastly, Sir, the *Comédie Française* has discarded this custom, not from caprice but from reason. It has been realised that these lifeless and imperfect ghosts of beautiful nature were opposed to truth and the perfection of comedies.

Opera, which of all kinds of entertainment is that which most nearly approaches that of the Greeks, has adopted masks for the dance alone, a convincing proof that no one has ever suspected this art capable of speech. If one had imagined that this art could imitate, one would have been well advised not to give it a mask and to deprive it of the most useful aid to speaking without words, and the lively expression of the soul's emotions revealed by exterior signs.

Let us continue to dance as at present, let ballets be used in opera only to give time for the actors to recover their breath, let ballets be no more interesting than the monotonous *entr'actes* in comedies ; one could then, without danger, preserve the use of these mournful masks, which are not to be preferred to the face of a corpse. But if art is to be perfected, if dancers are eager to depict and imitate, then we must abandon masks and break their moulds. Nature cannot be associated with a clumsy art, and whatever eclipses and degrades it must be forbidden by the enlightened artist.

It is as difficult, Sir, to trace the origin of masks, as it is to form a proper idea of the entertainments and dances of the ancients. This art, like a great many precious things, has been, as it were, entombed in the ruins of antiquity. There still exist faint outlines of many beauties, to which each author lends different features and colours ; each writer endows them with the character which most flatters his taste and intelligence. The continual contradictions which exist in these works, so far from enlightening us, only re-plunge us into our first obscurity. Antiquity, in certain respects, is a chaos impossible for us to unravel, it is a world the immensity of which is unknown to us ; everyone boasts of being able to travel in it without losing his way.   The multitude of things presented to us at so great a distance away is shown in too narrow a perspective.   The eye loses it and can only faintly distinguish objects.   But imagination comes to our aid, shortens the distance and strengthens the weakness of our sight ; enthusiasm brings objects closer, it creates new ones of them, it makes monsters of them, everything appears larger under its influence.   Here one might well apply those verses of Molière from *Les Femmes Savantes :*—

...... j'ai vu clairement des hommes dans la lune,

> *   *   *   *   *

Je n'ai point encor vu d'hommes, comme je crois ;
Mais j'ai vu des clochers tout comme je vous vois ! [1]

Such is the vicissitude and unstability of things.   Arts as well as empires are subject to revolution ; what to-day shines with the greatest splendour, in a little while degenerates and falls into languor and profound obscurity.   However it may be (and in this respect opinions are one), the ancients spoke with their hands ; the atmosphere, temperament and application employed to perfect the art of gesture carried it to a degree of sublimity which we shall never attain unless we take the same pains to distinguish ourselves in this art as they did.   The dispute between Cicero and Roscius as to who should express thought best, Cicero by the turn and order of his phrases, or Roscius by the movements of his arms and expression of his face, prove very clearly that in this respect we are but children, since we have only mechanical and indeterminate movements, devoid of significance, character and life.

The ancients had arms and we have legs.   Let us unite to the beauty of our execution, Sir, the lively and animated expression of artists in pantomime ; let us destroy masks and gain a soul, and we shall be the best dancers in the world.

I am, &c.

[1] I have seen clearly men in the moon . . .
I have not yet seen men as I believe, but I have seen belfries as clearly as I see you !

LETTER X

I HAVE said, Sir, that dancing was too complicated, and
the symmetrical movements of the arms too uniform, for
the pictures to have variety, expression and simplicity ;
therefore, if we desire to approach our art in the light of
truth, let us give less attention to the legs and more to the
arms ; let us forsake *cabrioles* for the benefit of our gestures ;
perform less difficult steps and put more expression into
our faces ; not put so much energy into the execution, but
invest it with more expression ; let us gracefully set aside
the narrow laws of a school to follow the impressions of
nature and accord to dancing the soul and action which it
must possess in order to interest. By the word *action*,
I do not mean anything which only makes for bustle and
scurry, and a forcing of oneself to labour like a galley-slave
to jump, or depict a soul which one does not possess.

Action, in relation to dancing, is the art of transferring
our sentiments and passions to the souls of the spectators
by means of the true expression of our movements, gestures
and features. Action is simply pantomime. In the dancer
everything must depict, everything must speak ; each gesture,
each attitude, each *port de bras* must possess a different
expression. True pantomime follows nature in all her
manifold shades. If it deviate from her for an instant, the
pantomime becomes fatiguing and revolting. Students of
dancing should not confuse the noble pantomime of which
I speak with that low and trivial form of expression which
Italian players have introduced into France, and which
bad taste would appear to have accepted.

I believe, Sir, that the art of gesture is confined within
too restricted limits to produce great effects. The single
action of the right arm which is carried forward to describe
a quarter circle, while the left, which was in this position,

moves contrariwise in the same manner to be again extended, and form opposition with the leg, is not sufficient to express the passions ; so long as the movements of the arms are so little varied, they will never have the power to move or affect. In this respect the ancients were our masters, they understood the art of gesture far better than we, and it was only in this part of dancing that they went further than the moderns.   I grant with pleasure that they possessed what we lack, and what we shall possess when it pleases dancers to break away from the rules opposed to the beauty and spirit of their art.

The *port de bras* must be as varied as the different sentiments which dancing can express ; set rules become almost useless ; they must be broken and set aside at each moment, or, by following them exactly, the *port de bras* will be opposed to the movements of the soul, which cannot be limited to a fixed number of gestures.

The passions can be varied and sub-divided *ad infinitum*, and hence would require as many rules as there are modifications of them.   Where is the *maître de ballet* who would undertake such a task ?

Gesture is the countenance of the soul, its effect must be immediate and cannot fail to achieve its aim when it is true.

Instructed in the fundamental principles of our art, let us follow the movements of our soul ; it cannot betray us when it is subject to a lively feeling, and if at those moments it cause the arms to make such and such a gesture, this gesture is always just and correct and sure in its effect.   The passions are the springs which actuate the machine ; whatever movements result from it, they cannot fail to be expressive. After this, it cannot but be concluded that the sterile rules of a school must disappear from the *danse d'action* to give place to natural expression.

Nothing is so difficult to achieve as what is termed a pleasing grace ; it is good taste to make use of it and a fault to pursue and diffuse it everywhere alike.   The fewer the pretensions with which it is displayed, a studied negligence to conceal it, only renders it more piquant and affords it a new attraction.   Taste is the arbiter, it is that which affords graces their value and makes them pleasing ; if they be used without it they lose their names, charms and effect ; they become nothing more than affectation, the insipidity of which soon becomes insupportable.

It is not given to everybody to have taste, nature alone bestows it ; education refines and perfects it ; all the precepts that could be drawn up to produce it would be useless. It is either born with us or it is not. In the former case it will reveal itself, in the latter the dancer will be mediocre always.

It is the same with the movements of the arms ; a pleasing grace is to these what taste is to grace. It is impossible to succeed in pantomimic action without being also served by nature ; when she gives us our first lessons, progress is always rapid.

Let us conclude that action in dancing is too restrained, that charm and intelligence are not communicated to everyone equally, that taste and grace cannot be acquired. One can seek in vain to teach these qualities to those who were never born to have them—it is like sowing seed on stony ground. Many quacks pretend to do so, a still greater number of dupes follow their precepts, but all they learn is foolishness and the quacks have the profit.

The Romans, however, possessed schools where the art of saltation was taught, or, if you wish, that of gesture and gracefulness; but were the masters satisfied with their pupils ? Roscius was pleased with one only, who was doubtless gifted by nature; even then he always found something of which to complain.

Maîtres de ballet are persuaded that by gesture I understand the expressive movements of the arms, supported by striking and varied expressions of the features. But a dancer's arms will speak in vain if his face be unmoved. If the alteration in the features produced by the passions be not visible, if his eyes neither declare nor betray the sentiments with which he is swayed, then its expression is false, its play is mechanical and the resulting effect loses by the discord and defect of truth and verisimilitude.

I cannot better compare it than to what may be seen in masked balls, or in gaming-houses, but chiefly during carnival time at Venice. Imagine an immense table surrounded by a number of players all wearing masks more or less grotesque, but, in general, all simulating laughter. If we examine the faces alone, all the players

appear to be contented and satisfied ; it would be thought
that they were all winning.   But when the gaze is transferred
to their arms, attitudes and gestures, you see on one side
the fixed attention and uncertainty born of fear or hope ;
on another the impetuous movement of fury and spite,
a smiling mouth and a clenched fist which menaces heaven ;
in another case you hear awful curses issue from a mouth
apparently bursting with laughter ; in short, this contra-
diction of the features and the gestures produces an amazing
effect easier imagined than described.   Such is the
dancer whose face is expressionless, while his gestures
or steps manifest the lively sentiments with which he is
moved.

One cannot achieve distinction on the stage except one
be aided by nature; such was the opinion of Roscius.
According to him, says Quintilian, the art of pantomime
consists in gracefulness and the artless expression of the
sentiments of the soul; it knows no rules and cannot be
taught, nature alone bestows it.

To hasten the progress of our art and bring it nearer
the truth, we must sacrifice all our over-complicated steps ;
what is lost in regard to the legs will be gained in the arms,
the simpler the steps, the easier it will be to afford them
expression and grace.   Taste always flees from difficulties,
it is never found in conjunction with them.   Let dancers
keep them for study but banish them from execution, they
do not please the public at all, and only afford an indifferent
pleasure to those who realise the efforts required for them.
I regard a multiplication of difficulties in music and dancing
as a jargon which is absolutely foreign to them ; their
voices should be moving ; they should always speak from
the heart ; the language proper to them is that of sentiment,
which captivates everywhere because it is universally
understood by all nations.

A certain violinist is admirable, I am told ; that may
be, but he affords me no pleasure, does not soothe me,
produces no feeling in me at all.   He has a language, the
lover of music will answer me, which you do not understand ;
a conversation which it is not given to everyone to com-
prehend, he will continue ; but it is sublime for the one who
can understand and appreciate it, and its sounds are as many

sentiments which captivate and move when its language is understood.

So much the worse for this fine violinist, I shall tell him, if his merit be restricted to the affording of pleasure to a few. The arts are of all countries, let them assume a voice suitable to them; they have no need of interpretation, and will affect equally both the connoisseur and the ignoramus. If, on the contrary, their effect be limited to dazzling the eyes without moving the heart, without rousing the passions, without disturbing the soul, from that moment they will cease to be pleasing ; the voice of nature and the faithful expression of sentiment will always transport emotions into the least sensitive souls; pleasure is a tribute that the heart cannot refuse to the things which flatter and interest it.

Does a great Italian violinist arrive in Paris, everyone runs after him and no one listens to him ; however, everyone dubs him a miracle. The ears have not been soothed by his playing, the sounds have not affected the heart; but the eyes have been amused. His hand has skilfully passed from the neck of the instrument to its body, and his fingers have lightly run up and down the neck. The fingers have been as far as the bridge, he has accompanied these difficulties with a number of contortions which were so many invitations and seemed to imply : " Gentlemen, look at, but do not listen to me ; this is a diabolical passage, it will not be pleasing to your ears although it makes a fine noise, but I have been twenty years studying it." Applause bursts forth ; arms and fingers are deserving of praise ; and this numskull of a human machine is accorded what is constantly refused to a French violinist who to brilliancy of finger execution unites expression, intelligence, genius and the grace of his art.

For some time past, Italian dancers have taken the opposite view to the musicians. Being unable to enchant the sight, and not having inherited Fossan's pleasing ways, they make a great deal of noise with their feet by marking all the notes, so that one can look with admiration at the playing of the violinists of that nation and listen with pleasure to the dancing of their pantomimists. That was never the aim intended by the fine arts; they must paint, they must imitate, but with natural, simple and ingenious means. Taste does not exist in difficulties, it draws its charms from nature.

While taste is sacrificed to difficulties, while there is no reasoning so that dancing is made to consist of *tours de force* and tumbling, a low trade will be made of a charming art ; dancing, so far from making progress, will degenerate and again sink into obscurity, and I dare to say into the decline in which it was no more than a century ago.

It must not be understood from this that I seek to abolish the customary arm movements, all difficult and brilliant steps, and all the elegant positions in dancing ; I ask for more variety and expression in the arms, I wish to see them speak with more energy ; they express sentiment and voluptuousness, but this is not sufficient ; they have yet to depict fury, jealousy, spite, inconstancy, grief, vengeance, irony, all the passions of man which, in harmony with the eyes, features and gestures, will make me understand nature's sentiments. I desire also that the steps be arranged with intelligence and artistry, and that they correspond to the action and movements of the dancer's soul. I require that slow steps be not used in a lively scene, that there be no lively steps in a solemn scene, that in moments of vexation all those light steps, which should take place in a moment of inconstancy, should be avoided. Lastly, I require that they be not employed in moments of despair and discouragement ; then the features alone should depict, it is for the eyes to speak, the arms should even be motionless, and the dancer in these kinds of scenes will never be so excellent as when he does not dance or when his dance does not appear to be one. It is then that the *maître de ballet's* imagination should come into play. All my views, all my ideas tend only to the well-being and advantage of young dancers and *maîtres de ballet ;* let them weigh my ideas carefully, let them devise a new style, then they will see that all that I advance can be put into practice and achieve universal applause.

As for positions, everyone knows that there are five of them. It is even made out that there are ten, divided singularly enough into good and bad ones, into true and false ones. The number is of no account, and I shall not contest it. I shall simply say that these positions are good to know and better still to forget, and that it is the art of the great dancer to neglect them gracefully. Besides, all those positions in which the body is firm and well displayed are excellent. I know of no bad ones except those where the body is ill-posed so that it totters and the legs cannot support it. Those who are attached to the alphabet of their profession will treat me as a reformer and a fanatic. But I shall send them again to an art school and ask them whether they approve or condemn the pose of the handsome gladiator and that of Hercules. Do they disapprove ? I have gained my case; they are blind. Do they approve ? Then they have failed, because I shall prove that the poses of these two statues, masterpieces of antique art, are not those adopted by the technique of the dance.

The majority of those who adopt the theatrical profession imagine that to become a dancer it is sufficient to possess legs, to be an actor a good memory is the only essential, and to be a singer a voice is the sole requisite. Commencing from so false a premise, the first concentrate on stirring their legs, the second on exerting their memories, and the third on giving vent to cries or sounds. They are astonished that after many years of weary toil they are accounted detestable ; but it is impossible to succeed in an art without studying its principles, without penetrating its spirit and without feeling its effects. A good engineer will not seize on the feeblest works of a fortified place, if they be commanded by heights defended by men able to dislodge him. The sole means of achieving his aim is to make himself master of the principal defences and to carry them, because those which are weaker will then only be able to offer a feeble resistance or must themselves surrender. There are arts like fortified places and artists who resemble engineers. It is not a question of skimming the surface of the art, it must be probed to its depths. It is not enough to apply oneself to the minor details, for to seize upon superficial things only is to degenerate into mediocrity and obscurity.

I will make an average man into an average dancer, provided he be passably well made. I will teach him how to move his arms and legs, to turn his head. I will give him steadiness, brilliancy and speed ; but I cannot endow him with that fire and intelligence, those graces and that expression of feeling which is the soul of true pantomime. Nature was always superior to art, it is not for her to perform miracles.

The defect in wisdom and taste which exists among the majority of dancers is due to the bad education which they generally receive. They adopt the theatrical profession less to distinguish themselves in it than to throw off the yoke of dependency, less to escape a more tranquil profession than to enjoy the pleasures they think to encounter at each moment in the one they embrace ; in the flush of enthusiasm they see only the rosy side of the fame they desire to acquire. They learn dancing with fury, their taste diminishes in proportion to the difficulties they encounter, and which they themselves multiply. They apply themselves only to the material side of their art, they learn to jump more or less high, they strive mechanically to execute a number of steps, and, like children who utter a great many words devoid of sense and relation, they execute many phrases of steps devoid of taste and grace.

This infinite medley of steps more or less ill-combined, this difficult execution, these complicated movements deprive, as it were, dancing of speech. The more simplicity, softness and mellowness in the dancer's movements, the greater will be his facility to depict and express. He should divide his attention between the mechanism of steps and the movements proper to express the passions. Then dancing, liberated from minor details, would be able to devote itself to those of importance. It is an established fact that the breathlessness which results from such painful labour deprives the dancer of his power; that *entrechats* and *cabrioles* spoil the character of beautiful dancing; and that it is morally impossible to put soul, truth and expression into movements, while the body is ceaselessly convulsed by violent and reiterated jerks, and while the brain is concentrated on preserving the body from the accidents and falls which continually threaten it.

One should not be astonished to find more intelligence and facility of expression among players than dancers.

The majority of the former generally receive a better
education than the latter, besides, their profession leads
them to a type of study suitable to afford them a knowledge
of the world and the manners of polite society, the desire
for self-education and increase of knowledge beyond the
limits of the theatrical art. They take to literature. They
are acquainted with the works of poets and historians, and
several of them have proved by their writings that to an
ability to speak well they unite that of writing agreeably ;
if all these kinds of knowledge be not exactly analogous
to their profession, they nevertheless contribute to its
perfection. Of two players equally gifted by nature, the
one that will appear to the best advantage will undoubtedly
be he who puts the most intelligence and artlessness into
his acting.

Dancers, like players, should devote themselves to
depict and feel, they have the same object to attain. If
they be not really moved by the part they have to fill,
they cannot present the character with any degree of truth,
and they cannot hope to succeed and please ; they must
likewise captivate the public by the force of the illusion
and make it experience all the emotions by which they
are swayed. That realism, that enthusiasm which distinguishes the great actor and which is the life-blood of the
fine arts is, if I may so express myself, like an electric
spark. It is a fire which spreads rapidly, and in a moment
captivates the imagination of the spectator, stirring his soul
and rendering his heart susceptible to every emotion.

The voice of nature and the true movements of pantomimic action should be equally effective, the former attacks
the heart through the hearing, the latter through the sight ;
each of them makes an equally strong impression provided
that the thoughts expressed in mime be as lively, as striking,
and as animated as those rendered by speech.

It is impossible to create this interest by reciting
mechanically some beautiful verses and merely executing
some beautiful steps ; the soul, features, gestures and
attitudes must all speak at once and always with energy
and truth. Does the spectator put himself in the actor's
place, if the latter do not take that of the hero he portrays ?
Can he hope to move and cause tears to flow, if he do not

shed them himself ? Will his condition arouse sympathy, if he do not make it affecting and be not himself greatly moved by it ?

Perhaps you will tell me that players have over dancers the advantage of speech, the force and power of discourse. But have not the latter gestures, attitudes, steps and music, which are to be regarded as the organ and interpreter of the dancer's successive movements ?

In order that our art may arrive at that degree of the sublime which I demand and hope for it, it is imperative for dancers to divide their time and studies between the mind and the body, and that both become the object of their application ; but, unfortunately, all is given to the latter and nothing to the former. The legs are rarely guided by the brain, and, since intelligence and taste do not reside in the feet, one often goes astray. The man of intelligence disappears, there remains nothing but an ill-ordered machine given up to the sterile admiration of fools and the just contempt of connoisseurs.

Let us study then, Sir, let us cease to resemble marionettes, the movements of which are directed by clumsy strings which only amuse and deceive the common herd. If our souls determine the play and movement of our muscles and tendons, then the feet, body, features and eyes will be stirred in the right manner, and the effects resulting from this harmony and intelligence will interest equally the heart and the mind.

I am, &c.

LETTER XI

IT is rare, Sir, not to say impossible, to find men perfectly proportioned, and for this reason it is quite common to meet with a crowd of ill-proportioned dancers, in whom one only too often sees defects of physique which all the resources of art can scarcely conceal. Is this due to a fatality of human nature by which we always withdraw from that which is suited to us, and so often pursue a career in which we can neither advance nor succeed ? It is this blindness, this ignorance concerning ourselves, that produces such a multitude of bad poets, of mediocre painters, of tedious players, of noisy musicians, of detestable dancers and mummers, in short, Sir, of impossible people in every art. These same men put in suitable posts might have been useful, but, away from their proper occupation and station, their real talents are wasted and exchanged for ones which vie with each other in absurdity.

When one wishes to enter into the dancing profession, the first consideration to be taken is that of physique, provided that the postulant has attained an age at which he should be capable of reflection. If his natural defects be irremediable, he must renounce at once, and completely, the thought conceived of the advantage of competing in the pleasures of others. Should these defects be capable of remedy by care, constant exercise, and by the counsel and advice of a well-informed and enlightened teacher, then it is imperative not to neglect a single effort which can remedy the imperfections over which he desires to triumph. He must look forward to the time when his body has attained its greatest strength and stability, that is to say, its full growth ; and when his desire to conquer his defects has been strengthened by so long and inveterate a habit that it can no longer be destroyed.

Unfortunately there are few dancers capable of this stringent self-examination. Some, blinded by self-esteem, imagine themselves to be faultless; others shut their eyes to those defects which the most cursory examination would reveal to them. Again, if they disregard what every man of intelligence has the right to reproach them with, it is not astonishing that they fail to achieve their aim. The disproportion of the limbs ceaselessly opposes the play of the muscles and the harmony which should make a perfect whole. There is no more union in the steps; no more softness in the movements: no elegance in the attitudes and oppositions: no proportion in the *déploiements* and consequently no firmness and no equilibrium. To that point, Sir, has been brought the execution of the dancers who are blind to their physique and who fear to examine themselves when they study and execute their exercises. We can, without offending them, give them their just due and call them bad dancers.

Probably, were good masters more common, good pupils would not be so scarce; but the masters who are fit to teach do not give lessons, and those who ought to take them are eager to give lessons to others. What shall we say of the careless uniformity of their teaching? One will cry, "There is only one correct method of teaching." I agree, but is there only one way of pointing this out and passing it on to pupils one likes, and is it not essential to lead them to the same end but by different roads? I acknowledge that to succeed in it one must have a particular sagacity, for, without reflection and study, it is impossible to apply principles according to the different types of conformation and the various degrees of aptitude; one cannot see at a glance what is expedient for one, what is not suitable for another, and lastly one can never vary the lessons in proportion to the different varieties which nature or habit, the latter often more rebellious than nature even, offer and present us.

It is then essentially the master's right to place each pupil in the class suitable to him. For this purpose it is not sufficient to possess only the most exact knowledge of the art, it is also necessary to guard against that vain pride which inclines each one to think that his own method of execution is the best and the only one which can please ; because a master who always regards himself as a model of perfection and devotes himself only to making of his pupils a copy of which he is the good or bad original, will not succeed in making even tolerable ones, except he encounter those who are gifted with the same disposition as he, and who have the same height, the same conformation, the same intelligence, and, lastly, the same aptitude.

Among faults of physical construction, I generally notice two principal ones ; one is to be *jarreté*,[1] the other is to be *arqué*.[2] These two defects of conformation are almost universal and differ only in their degree ; we see very few dancers free from one or the other.

A dancer is said to be *jarreté* when his hips are narrow and turned inwards, his thighs are close together, his knees are large and so close to each other that they touch and almost adhere, while his feet are quite apart from each other so that the space between the knees and the feet almost resembles the figure of a triangle ; further, I remark an enormous bulge in the inner surface of his ankles, while his instep is higher than usual, and his tendon Achilles is not only slender and puny, but very far from the joint.

A dancer who is *arqué* is one in whom the contrary defect is noticed. This defect continues from the hip to the foot, for these parts describe a line which gives the figure some resemblance to a bow ; in fact the hips are broad, the thighs and knees well apart, so that the light that should naturally be seen between some of the portions of the lower limbs when closed, is seen all the way down and appears wider than it should be. Persons so constructed have in addition a long and flat foot, the outside of the ankle projecting, and the tendon Achilles large and near the joint.

These two diametrically opposed defects prove with greater force than any rhetoric that the lessons suitable for the first would be harmful to the second, and that the studies of two dancers as different in height as in physical structure, cannot be the same. The one who is *jarreté* must continually devote himself to separating those parts pressed too closely together. The first method of succeed-

[1] Literally, *gartered*.
[2] Literally, *arched*.

ing in this is to turn the thighs well outwards and to move
them in this direction, while profiting by the liberty of the
rotary movement of the femur in the cotyloid cavity of the
hip-bones. Aided by this exercise, the knees will follow
the same direction and return, as it were, to their place.
The knee-cap, which seems intended to limit the flexion
of the knee too far behind the joint, will fall perpendicularly
over the point of the foot, and the thigh and leg, being in
the same line, will thus describe a perpendicular which
will assure the firmness and stability of the body.

The second remedy to employ is to maintain a continual
movement in the knee joints, so that they appear extremely
stretched without actually being so. That, Sir, is a work
of time and habit; when this habit is strongly contracted,
it is impossible for the joint to retake its natural and vicious
position without efforts which cause in those parts an
insupportable numbness and pain. I have known dancers
who have discovered the art of concealing this defect to
such a degree that it would never be noticed if the straight
entrechat and very strong *temps* had not betrayed them.
This is the reason: the muscular contraction resulting
from the efforts of jumping, tightens the joint and forces
each part to go back into its place and return to its natural
form. The knees, thus forced, are carried inwards, they
reassume their normal size, which offers an obstacle to
the beats of the *entrechat ;* the more these parts come
together, the more those which are beneath them are
separated ; the legs, being unable either to beat or to cross,
remain as if motionless at the moment of the action of the
knees which roll disagreeably one on the other, and the
entrechat being neither *coupé*, nor *battu*, nor *croisé* by the
step, cannot have the speed and brilliancy which are its
merit. Nothing is more difficult, in my opinion, than to
conceal these defects, above all in vigorous movements where
the whole body is shaken and sustains violent and reiterated
jerks, giving itself to contrary movements and to continual
and varied efforts. If art then can triumph over nature,
of what praise is not the dancer worthy ?

He who is thus constructed should renounce *entrechats*,
cabrioles and all difficult and complicated steps, with all
the more reason that his execution will certainly be feeble,

because his hips being narrow, or, to employ the language of anatomy, the pelvic bones being less wide, they allow less play to the muscles which are attached to them and on which the movements of the body partly depend ; movements and flexions much more easy when these same bones are much wider, because then the muscles end or start from a point further distant from the centre of gravity. However that may be, the *danse noble* and *terre à terre* is the only one suitable to such dancers. Besides, Sir, what dancers who are *jarretés* lose in strength, they seem to gain in grace. I have noticed that they were soft and brilliant in the most simple things, easy in difficulties which did not require efforts beyond their powers, and that their beats are always graceful because they make use of, and profit by, the bones and tendons which move the instep. These are the qualities which compensate them for the strength they lack ; and, in matters of dancing, I always prefer skill to strength.

Those who are *arqués* have only to apply themselves to bringing together those parts which are too separated, to diminishing the space which is found principally between the knees. They have no less need than the others of the exercise which turns out the thighs, and it is less easy for them to conceal their defects. In general, they are strong and vigorous ; consequently they have less suppleness in the muscles and their joints move less easily. It can be understood that if this defect in physique arise from the deformity of the bones, all labour would be useless and the efforts of art powerless.

I have said that dancers who are *jarretés* should maintain a little flexion in their execution, the former from the opposite cause should be fully stretched and cross their *temps* more narrowly so that the union of the parts can diminish the light or interval which naturally separates them. They are sinewy, lively and brilliant in things which demand strength rather than skill ; sinewy and light, considering the direction of their groups of muscles, and considering the consistency and resistance of their articular ligaments ; lively, because they cross rather low than high, and, having for this reason less distance to go to beat the *temps*, they pass them with more speed ; brilliant, because of the light

between the parts which cross and uncross. This light,
Sir, is exactly the *chiaroscuro* of the dance, because, if the
beats of the *entrechat* be neither cut nor beaten, but, on the
contrary, rubbed or rolled one on the other, there will
not be the light which gives value to shadows, and the
legs, too close together, will offer only an indistinct and
ineffectual mass. They have little skill because they rely
too much on their strength, and this same strength is
opposed to their suppleness and ease. If their strength
leave them for an instant, they are clumsy; they ignore
the art of concealing their state by using simple *temps* which,
requiring little effort, always give them the time to regain
their strength; moreover, they have very little elasticity
and rarely strike with the toe.

I believe I have discovered the true reason for this when
I consider the long and flat shape of their feet. I compare
this part to a lever of the second order, that is to say, a
lever where the weight is between the fulcrum and the
power, so that the fulcrum and the power are at its extremities. Hence the fixed point or fulcrum corresponds to
the extremity of the foot, the resistance or weight of the
body is carried on the instep, and the power which raises
and sustains this weight is applied to the heel by means of
the tendon Achilles. Now as the lever is stronger in a
foot that is long and flat, the weight of the body is further
distant from the fulcrum and nearer the power; hence the
weight of the body must be greater and the strength of the
tendon Achilles diminish in equal proportion. I have
said then that this weight not being in as exact a proportion
in dancers that are *arqués* as it is in those who are *jarretés*,
who have usually a high and strong instep, the former have
necessarily less ease in raising themselves on the extremity
of the toes.

I have observed again, Sir, that defects encountered from
the hips to the feet make themselves felt from the shoulder
to the hand, more often the shoulder follows the conformation
of the hips; the elbow that of the knee; the wrist that of
the foot. A little attention will convince you of this truth,
and you will observe that, in general, defects of physique,
resulting from the vicious arrangement of certain joints,
are common to all. This principle accepted, the teacher

should suggest different movements of the arms to different pupils. This care is most important; short arms require only movements proportionate to their length, long arms cannot lose their extent except by the roundness given them. Art consists in taking advantage of these imperfections, and I know dancers who, by means of the *effacements* of the body, skilfully conceal the length of their arms; they make a portion of them recede into the shadow.

I said that dancers who are *jarretés* are feeble, they are thin and slender; dancers who are *arqués* are more vigorous, they are big and sinewy. It is a common failing to think that a man who is big and thick-set must be heavy; this principle is true as regards the actual weight of the body, but it is false in what concerns dancing, because lightness is born solely of the strength of the muscles. Every man who is only feebly aided by them will always " fall " heavily. The reason is simple, the weak parts being unable to resist the stronger parts at the moment of the fall (that is to say, the weight of the body which acquires, according to the height from which it falls, a new degree of weight), give way and bend. It is in this moment of relaxation and flexion that the noise of the fall is heard, a noise which diminishes considerably and which can even pass unnoticed when the body can maintain itself in an exactly perpendicular line, and when the muscles and tendons have vigour enough to oppose the falling weight and to resist vigorously the shock which might cause them to give way.

Nature has not spared the fair sex from the imperfections which I have mentioned to you, but artifice and the fashion of petticoats have happily come to the aid of our *danseuses*. The panier conceals a multitude of defects, and the curious glance of the critics cannot rise high enough to pass judgment. Most *danseuses* dance with the knees separated, as if they were naturally *arqués*. Thanks to this bad custom and to petticoats, they appear more brilliant than the men, because, as I have said, beating only with the lower part of the leg, they pass their *temps* quicker than the latter, who, concealing nothing from the spectator, are obliged to beat theirs with stretched muscles and to make them come chiefly from the hip. You understand that it takes

more time to move a whole than a part.   As to the brilliancy
which *danseuses* evince, vivacity contributes to it, but less,
however, than the petticoats, which, concealing their defects
of physique, fix the looks of the spectators more attentively.
All the vigour of the *battements* being, as it were, brought
to one point, they appear livelier and more brilliant ; the
eye can take it all in at a glance, which is the more concentrated the smaller the space it has to traverse.

Besides, Sir, a pretty face beautiful eyes, an elegant
form and voluptuous arms, are the inevitable rocks on
which criticism founders, and powerful claims to the indulgence of the spectator, whose imagination substitutes for
the pleasure which he has not received, that pleasure
which he might possess off the stage.

I am, &c.

IN order to dance well, Sir, nothing is so important as
the turning outwards of the thigh; and nothing is so
natural to men as the contrary position ; we are born
thus, and it is useless, in order to convince you of this
truth, to quote as examples the Levantines, Africans, and
all races given to dancing or rather leaping, or other forms
of vigorous exercise. Without going so far, consider
children ; glance at the inhabitants of the countryside,
and you will observe that all of them have their feet turned
inwards. The contrary position, then, is a purely conventional one, and an unequivocal proof that this defect
is only imaginary is that a painter would err as much against
nature as against the principles of his art, if he placed his
model with the feet turned outwards like those of a dancer.
You see then, Sir, that to dance elegantly, to walk gracefully
and to carry oneself nobly, it is imperative to reverse the
order of things and force the limbs, by means of an exercise
both long and painful, to take a totally different position
from that which is natural to them.

It is impossible to bring about this change, of such
vital importance in our art, without taking it in hand in
the days of childhood ; that is the only time when success
is possible because then all the limbs are supple and may
easily be made to take the desired position.

A skilful gardener would certainly not think of trying
to train the branches of an old tree ; they would be too
brittle to bend and would break sooner than grow in the
desired direction. He must take a young sapling which
he will easily train to take whatever shape he desires ;
its tender branches will bend and twist at his pleasure ;
time, in strengthening its boughs, will fix them in the
direction planned by the master's hand, and each of

them will remain for ever in the position designed by art.

You see, Sir, there you have an example of a change in natural condition, but this operation once achieved, it is impossible for art to effect a second miracle by restoring the tree to its original state ; nature in certain forms will only submit to changes provided she be still weak. If time have given her strength she resists, she is indomitable.

Let us conclude that parents are, or, at least should be, the first teachers of their children. How many defects do we not encounter among those confided to our care ? One will say : " It is the nurse's fault." Such feeble arguments and frivolous excuses, so far from justifying the negligence of fathers and mothers, only serve to condemn them. Supposing the children have been badly swathed, it is an additional reason to arouse their attention, because it is certain that two or three years' negligence on the part of the nurses can be of no avail against eight or nine years of the parents' care.

But let us return to the turned-in position. A dancer with his limbs turned inwards is awkward and disagreeable. The contrary attitude gives ease and brilliancy, it invests steps, positions and attitudes with grace.

It is difficult to succeed in turning one's limbs outwards, because the means proper to employ for this purpose are often ignored. Most young people who take up dancing think that they will succeed in this by forcing outwards their feet only. I know that the foot lends itself to this treatment by reason of its suppleness, and the elasticity of its articulation with the leg ; but this method is the more false since it displaces the ankles and does not affect either the knees or the thighs.

Again, it is impossible to turn the foot outwards without the help of the knee, which, in fact, has two movements only, that of flexion and that of extension : the former determines the backward movement of the leg, the second the forward movement of the leg. Again, the knees cannot be carried outwards by themselves, all depends essentially on the thigh, since it is that which controls the parts which it dominates and which are below it, consequently it turns them by a rotary movement with which it is endowed, and, in whatever direction it moves, the knee, leg and foot are compelled to follow it.

I shall not speak to you of an ill-conceived and ill-arranged machine called the *tourne-hanche*,[1] which, far from being efficacious, cripples those who make use of it by forcing the waist to take on a much more disagreeable defect than the one it is desired to eliminate.

The simplest and most natural means are always those which reason and common sense should prescribe, when they are sufficient ; in order to be well turned outwards it is sufficient to practise a moderate but regular exercise. *Ronds de jambe en dehors* and *en dedans*, and *battements tendus* working from the hip, are the sole exercises to follow. Almost imperceptibly they give play, spring and suppleness, while on the other hand the *tourne-hanche* only gives rise to movements more indicative of constraint than of liberty.

Is it possible that by cramping the fingers of any instrumentalist he will be made to acquire a lively execution and a brilliant cadence ? No, undoubtedly, it is only the free use of the hand and the joints which can procure him that speed, brilliancy and precision which are the essence of fine execution. How then can a dancer hope to succeed in attaining these perfections if he pass half his life in fetters ? Yes, Sir, the use of that machine is pernicious. It is not by violence that an innate defect is corrected ; it is by time, study and application.

There are still persons who begin too late, and who take up dancing at an age when they should be renouncing it. You understand that in such circumstances machines will be no more efficacious than continual exercises.

I have known men who gave themselves a painful experience, since, their muscles being set, they were deprived of that suppleness which is the privilege of youth. A defect of thirty-five years' standing is an old one, the time has passed for it to be changed or remedied.

These defects born of habit are innumerable. I see every child occupied in some way in disarranging and disfiguring his physique; some displace the ankles through the habit they have contracted of standing on one leg only and playing, as it were, with the other ; placing it in a position

[1] Literally *hip-turner*.

which, though disagreeable and strained, does not fatigue them, because the softness of their tendons and muscles lend themselves to all kinds of movement. Others spoil their knees by the attitudes which they adopt in preference to those which are natural to them. One, owing to a habit by which he holds himself obliquely and pushes one shoulder forward, displaces a shoulder blade. Another, repeating at each moment a movement in a cramped position, throws his body all to one side and comes to have one hip larger than the other.

I should never conclude were I to speak to you of all the misfortunes which have their origin in the faulty carriage of the body. All these defects, mortifying for those who have contracted them, cannot be remedied except in their early stages. A habit born in childhood is strengthened in youth, becomes deeply rooted in manhood, and is incurable in old age.

Dancers, Sir, should follow the same regimen as athletes and adopt the same precautions which the latter employ when they go to wrestle and box ; this care would preserve them from accidents which happen to them daily : accidents on the stage, as numerous as *cabrioles*, which increase in proportion as nature is outraged and forced to execute actions generally far beyond her strength. If our art demand bodily strength and agility as well as qualities of the mind, what pains must we not take to acquire a sound constitution ! To be a good dancer, one must be temperate. Would English thoroughbreds (if I may be permitted the comparison) have that speed and agility which distinguishes and makes them preferred to all other breeds, if they were less well-cared for ? Everything they eat is weighed with the greatest exactitude, everything they drink is scrupulously measured ; the duration of their exercise is fixed as well as that of their rest. If these precautions be effective with robust animals, how much more will a careful and regular life influence those beings naturally weak but destined for a violent and painful exercise, which requires the strongest and most robust constitution ?

The breaking of the dancer's tendon Achilles and the leg, the dislocation of his foot, in fine, the dislocation of any part, is commonly caused by one of three things. First,

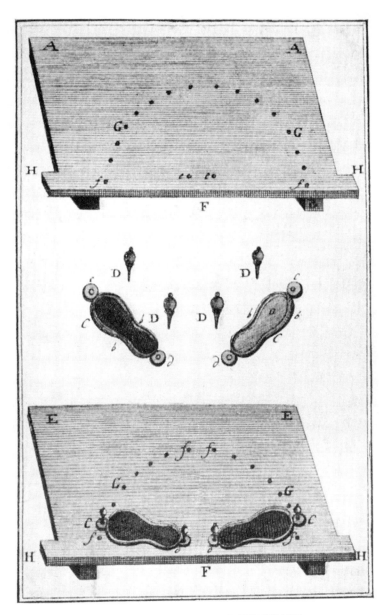

THE TOURNE HANCHE, OR HIP TURNER

*From Mereau's "Reflexions sur le Maintien et sur les Moyens
d'en Corriger tous les Défauts," 1760*

by unevenness in the stage, by an improperly fastened trap, by some tallow or similar substance which, being trodden on, often occasions his fall. Secondly, by a too violent or too lengthy exercise which, added to excesses of another kind, enfeebles and relaxes the limbs, so there is little suppleness, the muscles have only a forced action, and all is brittle. This rigidity in the muscles, this lack of vital juices, and this exhaustion lead to the most fatal accidents. Thirdly, by want of skill and by all the bad habits contracted during exercise, and by the faulty positions of the feet which, never being pointed downwards when the body comes to the ground, turn, bend or give way under the weight they are required to support.

The sole of the foot is the true base which supports the whole body. A sculptor would run the risk of destroying his work if he supported it on a round and moving body. The fall of his statue would be inevitable, for it would infallibly snap and break. For the same reason the dancer must make use of all the toes of his feet as so many branches of which the spreading out on the ground will increase the size of his base, consolidate and maintain his body in a fit and proper equilibrium. If he neglect to spread his toes out, if he do not grip the stage in such a manner as to keep himself firm, a multitude of accidents will happen to him. The foot will lose its natural shape, it will become round and roll from side to side from the little toe to the big toe, and *vice versa*. This kind of rolling, caused by the convex form taken by the extremity of the foot in this position, is opposed to all stability. The ankles are unsteady and displaced, and you feel, Sir, that, at the moment when the body falls from a height and is unable to find a certain point capable of supporting and breaking its fall, all the joints will be shaken by the shock ; and the moment when the dancer attempts to find a firm position, and when he makes the most violent efforts to escape the danger of this shock, will always be the one when he will give way as the result of a sprain or the breaking of a leg or tendon. The sudden change from relaxation to a strong tension, and from flexion to a violent extension, is the cause then of a shoal of accidents which would doubtless be less frequent if dancers prepared themselves against falls, and if the weak parts did not attempt to resist a weight which they could neither support nor overcome. One cannot warn dancers too much against false positions since their consequences are fatal.

Falls caused by unevenness in the stage and other similar things cannot be attributed to our want of skill. As for those which proceed from our weakness and prostration after an excess of physical exercise and as the result of a style of living which culminates in exhaustion, such accidents cannot be prevented except by a change of life and by exercise duly proportioned to our strength. The ambition to perform *cabrioles* is a mad one which leads nowhere. A buffoon arrives from Italy ; immediately the dancers wish to imitate the ease of his leaps ; the weakest are always those who put forth the greatest efforts to equal and even surpass him. One might say, on seeing our dancers jigging, that they were stricken by some malady which needed great leaps and enormous gambols to cure it. I liken them, Sir, to the frog in the fable, who burst while making efforts to blow herself out, and dancers break and strain their limbs in endeavour to emulate the strong and muscular Italian.

An author, whose name escapes me, committed a gross error by inserting in a book, which will always reflect honour on our nation and our age, that the body was raised by the flexion and extension of the knees. This principle is totally false, and you will be convinced of the physical impossibility of this if you bend your knees and then straighten them again. Whether these different movements be executed quickly or slowly, gently or vigorously, the feet will not leave the ground ; flexion or extension cannot raise the body if the parts essential to the movement be not brought into play. It would have been wiser to say that the action of jumping depends on the muscles of the instep and on the tendon Achilles if they worked by percussion ; because one would gain a slight elevation without recourse to flexion and consequently without bending the knees.

It would be still another error to persuade oneself that a strong and vigorous man must be able to spring higher than a weak and slender one ; experience teaches us every day the contrary. We observe some dancers who cut their *temps* strongly, who beat them vigorously and firmly, and who yet, however, attain only a slight elevation, reckoning perpendicularly. I say perpendicularly to distinguish it from an oblique or sideway elevation. This is, if I may use the expression, a sham effect dependent solely on skill. On the other hand we have weak men whose execution is less muscular, more correct than strong, more adroit than vigorous, who have a prodigious elevation. Hence, Sir, the power to elevate the body is primarily dependent on the shape of the foot and the length of the tendon and its elasticity; the knees, loins and arms contribute together to this action. The stronger the pressure, the greater the rebound, and consequently the higher the elevation.

The flexion of the knees and their extension share in the movements of the instep and tendon Achilles, which must be regarded as the essential sources of power. The muscles of the body assist this operation and maintain the body in a perpendicular line, while the arms which have imperceptibly contributed to the total effect of all parts serve, as it were, as wings and counterpoise to the machine. Consider, Sir, all those animals furnished with thin and lengthy tendons— deer, roebuck, sheep, cats, monkeys and so on—and you will notice that these animals have a speed and ease of elevation which differently constructed animals do not possess.

It is generally believed that the legs beat the *temps* of the *entrechat* as the body comes to the ground. I admit that the eyes often deceive us, not having proper time for examination, but logic and reflection reveal to us what speed does not permit to be analysed. This error arises from the quickness with which the body falls, although actually the *entrechat* is executed when the body has attained its highest point of elevation; the legs, during the imperceptible time taken to come to the ground, are preparing to sustain the shock which the weight of the body is about to produce; their immobility is imperative; if there were no interval between the " cuts " and the descent, how would the dancer come to the ground and what would be the position of his feet? If the possibility of beating during the descent be admitted, the interval necessary to the preparation for the fall is curtailed. Again, it is certain

that if the feet came to the ground at the moment when
the legs were still beating, they would not be disposed
ready to sustain the body, they would give way under
the weight which threatened to crush them, and could not
escape strain or dislocation.

Nevertheless, a great many dancers believe that they
execute the *entrechat* while descending, and consequently
many dancers are mistaken.   I do not say that it is morally
impossible to make a movement of the legs by a violent
effort of the hip, but a movement of this kind cannot be
considered as a *temps* of the *entrechat* or of the dance.
I have convinced myself of this fact, and it is only after
repeated experiments that I venture to combat an idea
which would never have gained credence, if the majority of
dancers did not confine themselves to using their eyes alone.

In fact, I have many times climbed on to a board, the
extremities of which were raised off the ground, when I
suddenly saw that the plank was about to be knocked from
beneath me.   Fear then forced me to make a movement,
which, to avoid a fall, raised me a little above the board
and made me describe an oblique instead of a straight line.
This action breaking my fall gave my legs the facility of
moving, because I was raised above the board, and half an
inch is space enough in which to beat an *entrechat* if one be
quick.

But if, without my being forewarned, the board were
broken or displaced, then I should drop perpendicularly ;
the weight of my body would fall on the lower parts, my
legs being motionless ; and my feet pointing directly
towards the ground would be immobile, but in a position
fit to receive and support the mass.

If one admit strength in the legs at the moment when
the body descends, and believe that it is possible to execute
the action a second time without a new effort and a new
point of support against which the feet push by a more or
less strong pressure, I shall ask why the same power does
not exist in a man who springs in order to jump a ditch ?
Why cannot he pass beyond the point he has fixed ?   Why,
I say, cannot he change in the air the estimate he has made
of the distance and the strength required to cross it ?
Finally, should his estimate be in error so that he is about

to fall in the water, why cannot he repeat the effort and carry his body beyond the ditch by a second jerk ? If it be impossible to make such a movement, how much more so is it to make another which requires grace, ease and tranquillity.

Every dancer who executes an *entrechat* knows how long he will take to beat it, imagination always outstrips the legs ; one cannot cut eight times if the intention is to beat six, without this precaution there would be as many falls as steps.

I submit then that the body cannot perform twice in the air when the springs of the machine have acted and their effect has been predetermined.

Two further defects oppose the progress of our art : first, the disproportions which commonly exist in the steps ; secondly, the want of firmness in the loins.

Disproportions in steps have their origin in the imitation and small reasoning power of dancers. The *déploiements* of the legs and *temps ouverts* were doubtless suitable for Dupré ; the elegance of his figure and the length of his limbs were wonderfully adapted to the execution of *temps développés* and difficult steps of his style. But what was suitable to him cannot be fit for dancers of mediocre stature. However, everyone wished to imitate him ; the shortest legs struggled to describe the same spaces and circles as those of that celebrated dancer ; there was no more stability ; the hips were never in place, the body shook unceasingly and the execution was ridiculous.

The reach and length of the limbs should determine the contours and *déploiements*, without this precaution there can be no harmony, no tranquillity and no grace ; the limbs ceaselessly disconnected and always apart will throw the body into false and disagreeable positions, and the dance, deprived of its true proportions, will resemble the action of those marionettes whose dislocated movements show nothing but a coarse caricature of the harmonious movements which good dancers ought to have.

This defect, Sir, is very common among those who dance in the serious style ; and as this kind of dancing is more fashionable in Paris than anywhere else, it is very usual to see a dwarf dance in a manner that would be ridiculous in anyone but a very tall man. I dare assert that those who are gifted with a majestic stature sometimes take advantage of the extent of their limbs and of the ease with which they can cover the stage and separate their *temps ;* these exaggerated *déploiements* spoil the staid and noble character which fine dancing should possess, and deprive the execution of its mellowness and softness.

The contrary of what I have just remarked offers a defect no less disagreeable. Mincing steps, poor and limited *temps*, in short, a confined manner of dancing, equally offend good taste. Then, I repeat, the stature and physique of the dancer should fix and determine the extent of his movements : and the proportions which his steps and attitudes should have in order to be executed correctly and brilliantly.

One cannot be an excellent dancer without being firm in the loins, even if one possess all the other qualities essential to the perfection of this art. It cannot be denied that this strength is a natural gift. Although it may be developed by the care of a clever master, yet this artificially gained strength is useless. We daily observe strong and vigorous dancers who have neither *aplomb* nor steadiness, and whose execution shows weakness in the loins. We see others who, on the contrary, not being endowed with this strength, are, so to speak, firmly fixed on the hips with a strong waist and ribs. In them, art has compensated for nature, because they have had the good fortune to meet with excellent masters who have shown them that, when the ribs are weak, it is impossible to maintain oneself perpendicularly ; that one's outline is in bad taste ; and that the weakness of that part of the body is inimical to *aplomb* and equilibrium. Such dancers possess a displeasing defect in the waist, and the weakness of the trunk takes away from the lower limbs the freedom they need in order to move easily. The body is unstable in its movements and often drags the legs with it. Being deflected from its centre of gravity, it only regains its equilibrium after contortions which are inconsistent with the graceful and harmonious movements of dancing.

That, Sir, is a faithful picture of the execution of those dancers whose backs are weak or who do not study how to make good use of them. To dance well, the body must be firm and steady, motionless and unshaken, during movements of the legs. If, on the contrary, the dancer allow his body to take part in the movements of the feet, he will make as many grimaces and contortions as he executes steps ; then the performance is devoid of repose, homogeneity, harmony, precision, firmness, *aplomb* and equilibrium ; finally, it is deprived of grace and nobility, the absence of which qualities renders dancing unpleasing.

A great many dancers believe that to be flexible and yielding is merely a question of bending the knees sufficiently, but they are unquestionably in error, because flexion carried too far makes dancing wooden. It is possible for movements to be as hard and jerky with flexion as without it. The reason for this is simple, natural and obvious, when it is realised that the dancer's beats and movements are exactly subordinated to the time and movements of the music. Commencing from this principle, there is no doubt that if the knees be bent lower than necessary, having regard to the music to which the dance is performed, the time drags, languishes and is lost. To regain this time which slow and excessive flexion has made the dancer lose, the extension must be quick, and it is this sudden passing from flexion to extension which gives the execution a jerkiness and hardness as irritating and as disagreeable as that which results from stiffness.

The yielding action depends partly on the proportionate flexion of the knees, but this movement is not sufficient, the instep must be elastic and the back serve, so to speak, as a counterpoise to the machine, in order that these springs may rise and fall gently. This rare harmony in every movement earned for the celebrated Dupré the title of " God of the Dance." In fact, this excellent dancer resembled a divinity rather than a man. The flexibility, suggestion of yielding, and gentleness with which all his movements were imbued, the exact interplay of all his muscles, offered an admirable whole. This harmony resulting from the fine physique, precise arrangement and well-combined proportion of every part, depending much less on study and reasoning than on nature, cannot be achieved except one be so endowed.

Even if the most mediocre dancers be acquainted with a great number of steps (truly ill-arranged and, for the most part, combined nonsensically and with bad taste), it is less common to find among them that accurate ear for time, a rare but inborn advantage which gives character to dancing, affords life and value to the steps, and invests every movement with vigour and animation.

There are ears which remain out of tune with, and insensible to, the most simple and most striking music ; there are a lesser number of them which feel the time, but cannot seize upon its niceties ; lastly, there are others which appreciate naturally and easily the movements of the most difficult melodies. Mlle. Camargo and M. Lany enjoyed that precious gift and that exact precision which accord to dancing a spirit of vivacity and gaiety which is never found in those dancers who have less sensitiveness and delicacy of hearing. It is, however, an established fact that the dancer's manner of taking his *temps* in contributing to his speed, adds in some degree to the delicacy of the ear. I mean that such a dancer can have a very delicate feeling and not reveal it to the spectator, if he do not possess the art of using with ease the tendons by which the instep is moved.

Unskilfulness then is opposed to accuracy, and a step which would have been striking and produced its effect, if it had been promptly taken at the end of a bar, appears cold and lifeless if all the parts move at once. It requires more time to move the whole machine than it does for a part. The flexion and extension of the instep is much more prompt and sudden than the general flexion and extension of all the muscles. This principle stated, precision is lacking in the person who, having an ear, does not know how to take his *temps* quickly.

The elasticity of the instep, and the more or less active play of its tendons, add to the natural sensitiveness of that part, and lend value and brilliancy to the dance. This charm, born of the harmony of the movements of the music with those of the dancer, captivates even those who have the least appreciative ear for music.

There are countries whose inhabitants enjoy that natural feeling for music, a quality which would be rare in France were Provence, Languedoc and Alsace not included among our provinces.

The Palatinate, Wurtemberg, Saxony, Brandenburg, Austria and Bohemia furnish the orchestras maintained by German princes with a number of excellent musicians and great composers. The Teutonic races are born with a lively and determined predilection for music; they have an innate sense of harmony, and nothing is more common than to hear accurately played concerts in the streets and tradesmen's shops. Each one sings his part and counts his time exactly; these concerts, directed by simple nature alone and executed by the poorest classes, have a unison which our French musicians would find difficult to emulate, despite the conductor's baton and the contortions of the person armed with it. This instrument, or rather this rod, betrays the schoolroom, reveals the weakness into which our music was plunged sixty years ago. Foreigners, accustomed to hear orchestras much larger than ours, containing a far greater range of instruments and infinitely richer in classical and difficult music, cannot accustom themselves to this baton, this sceptre of ignorance which was invented to guide beginners. This plaything of music in its cradle appears useless when this art has arrived at adolescence. The orchestra at the *Opéra* is undoubtedly the centre and meeting-place of skilled musicians, it is no longer necessary to warn them, as in former days, that there are flats in the key. I believe, Sir, that this instrument, doubtless useful in a period of ignorance, is no longer so in an age when the arts are nearing perfection. The disagreeable and harsh noise which the baton produces when the conductor, in a moment of enthusiasm, beats it on his desk, distracts the spectator's ear, disturbs the harmony, alters the singing of the melodies, and destroys the whole impression.

This natural and innate taste for music brings in its train a similar liking for dancing. These two arts are brothers and go hand-in-hand; the tender and harmonious accents of the former excite the agreeable and expressive movements of the latter; their combined effect offers animated pictures to our eyes and ears; these senses convey to the heart the interesting pictures which have moved them ; the heart in turn communicates these images to the soul, and the pleasure which results from the harmony and intelligence of these two arts captivates the spectator and makes him experience the most seductive pleasure.

Dancing is infinitely varied in all the provinces of Germany. The manner of dancing common to one village is almost entirely different from that of a neighbouring hamlet. Even the melodies used in their merry-making have a different character and movement, although they are all gay. Their dancing is seductive, because it is entirely of the soil ; their movements radiate only joy and pleasure ; and the precision with which they execute the dance affords a particular charm to their attitudes, steps and gestures. If it be a question of jumping, a hundred persons around an oak or a column take their time, rise and fall as one at the same moment. If the rhythm must be emphasised with a stamp of the foot, then all stamp together. If the women have to be lifted, they are seen all in the air at the same height, and they are not lowered except on the right note.

Counterpoint, which is undoubtedly the touchstone of the most delicate ear, presents the least difficulty to them : hence their dancing is animated and the delicacy of their ear invests their movements with a gusto and a variety never found in our French *contredanses*.

A dancer without an ear resembles a madman who talks ceaselessly and at random, with no sequence in his conversation, and who articulates disconnected words devoid of common sense. Words only serve to inform intelligent people of his madness and extravagance. The dancer with no ear, like the madman, makes ill-combined steps, and is always astray in his execution ; he continually runs after the time and never catches up with it. He hears nothing, everything is contrary in him ; his dancing has neither logic nor expression; and the music which should direct his movements, order his steps and determine his *temps*, serves only to betray his incapability and imperfections.

The study of music can, as I have told you already, remedy this defect and afford the organ of hearing more sensitiveness and accuracy.

I shall not give you, Sir, a long description of all the

enchaînements of steps associated with dancing. The detail would be immense ; besides, it would be useless for me to dilate on the technical side of my art. This part has been brought to so great a degree of perfection that it would be ridiculous to wish to give new precepts to dancers ; such a dissertation could not avoid being tedious and displeasing to you ; the legs should speak to the eyes and not to the ears.

I shall content myself then with stating that these *enchaînements* are innumerable, that each dancer has his particular manner of combining and varying his *temps*. Some dancing is like music, and some dancers resemble musicians. Our art is no richer in fundamental steps than music is in notes ; but we have octaves, semibreves, minims, crotchets, quavers, semiquavers and demi-semiquavers, beats to count and a bar to follow; this combination of a small number of steps and a small quantity of notes offers a multitude of *enchaînements* and varied features. Taste and genius always find a source of novelty in arranging and manipulating this small number of notes and steps in a thousand different ways. Slow and sustained steps, lively and hurried steps, *temps* more or less open, provide continual diversity.

I am, &c.

LETTER XIII

CHOREGRAPHY,[1] which you wish me to discuss with you, Sir, is the art of setting down dances by the aid of different signs, just as music is written down with the help of figures or characters called notes, with this difference, that a good musician will read two hundred bars in an instant, whereas an excellent *chorégraphe* will not decipher two hundred bars of dance notation in two hours. These representative signs are easily invented, easily learned and as easily forgotten. This manner of writing peculiar to our art, which the ancients probably ignored, was necessary from the first moment when dancing was ordered by rules. Professors used to send one another little *contredanses*, and brilliant and difficult dances, such as the *Menuet d'Anjou*, the *Bretagne*, the *Mariée*, and the *Passepied*, not counting the *Folies d'Espagne*, *Pavane*, *Courante*, *Bourrée d'Achille*, and the *Allemande*.

The tracks or figures of these dances were drawn, the steps were then indicated on the tracks by lines and conventional signs ; the cadence or bar was marked by little transverse lines which divided the steps and fixed the time. The air to which the dance was composed was noted at the top of the page, so that eight bars of choregraphic notation corresponded to eight bars of music. By means of this arrangement, one succeeded in spelling out the dance, provided that one took the precaution never to change the position of the book and to hold it always in the same direction. There, Sir, such was choregraphy formerly. Dancing was simple and not complicated, consequently

[1] In the 18th Century the art of dance notation was called choregraphy. This term is now generally applied to the art of dance composition, the recording of dances by means of lines and symbols being known as stenochoregraphy.

the method of writing it was simple, and one could learn to read it very easily.

But, nowadays, the steps are complicated, they are doubled and tripled, their inter-mixture is prodigious, it is then very difficult to note them in writing, and still more difficult to decipher them. Besides, this art is very imperfect; it indicates with exactitude the movements of the feet only, and if it shows us the movements of the arms, it orders neither the positions nor the contours they should have. Again, it shows us neither the attitudes of the body nor its *effacements*, nor the oppositions of the head, nor the different situations, noble and easy, necessary to each part. I regard it as a useless art, because it can do nothing for the perfection of our own. I would ask those who pride themselves on being inseparably devoted to choregraphy, and whom perhaps I scandalise, in what way that science has aided them? What lustre has it bestowed upon their talents, what distinction has it given to their reputation? They will reply, if they be sincere, that this art has not been able to raise them above what they were, but, on the other hand, they possess everything fine that has been done in the way of dancing for the last fifty years. "Preserve," I shall tell them, "this precious collection, lock up in your cabinet all that the Duprés, Camargos, Lanys, and perhaps even the Blondys, have imagined in *enchaînements* and subtle, bold and ingenious *temps;* this collection is doubtless very beautiful, but I see with regret that all this accumulation of riches has not saved you from being poor in what you should have drawn from your own capital. Hoard as much as it pleases you of these feeble monuments to the glory of our celebrated dancers; I see in them, and there will only be in them, the first sketch or the first thought of their talents. I shall only be able to distinguish scattered beauties without homogeneity and without colouring; the principal lines will be effaced, the proportions and agreeable contours will not impress my eyes; I shall perceive only the remains and tracing of a movement of the feet which will be accompanied neither by the attitudes of the body nor the positions of the arms, nor the expression of the heads; in short, you offer me only a canvas on which you have preserved some scattered lines by different masters."

I have learned choregraphy, Sir, and I have forgotten it ; if I think it useful for my progress, I shall learn it anew. The best dancers and the most celebrated *maîtres de ballet* disdain it because it is of no real help to them.   It could, however, acquire a measure of usefulness, and I propose to discuss it with you, after having acquainted you with a project born of some reflections on the *Académie de Danse*, whose establishment has had, in all probability, no other object than that of adorning the decadence of our art and of hastening its downfall.

Dancing and ballets would undoubtedly take on a new lease of life, if the customs established by a spirit of fear and jealousy did not in some way close the path of glory to all those who could appear with some advantage on the stage of the capital, and convince by the novelty of their style that genius is common to all countries, and springs up and develops in the provinces with as much ease as anywhere else.

Do not imagine, Sir, that I wish to disparage the dancers whom favour, or if you prefer, a propitious and favourable star, has elevated to a position to which their real talents entitled them.   Love of my art and not egotism is the only one which animates me ; and I am persuaded that, without wounding anyone, I should be allowed to claim for dancing the privileges enjoyed by comedy.   Now have not provincial actors the right to appear at Paris and to play there three different characters of their selection ?   " Yes, undoubtedly," I shall be told, " but they are not always welcomed."   What does it matter to the one who succeeds and pleases generally whether he be welcomed or not ? Every actor who, by means of his talents, triumphs over the players' faction, and who, without servility, attracts the unanimous approbation of an enlightened public, must be more than indemnified for the loss of a position which he regrets the less when he knows he truly deserves it.

Painting would certainly have not produced so many illustrious men in all the styles it includes, without that emulation which reigns in its academy.   There, Sir, genuine merit can fearlessly display itself ; it places each in the position suitable to him ; and in the Louvre Gallery favour was always weaker than a fine brush which compels it to silence.

If ballets be living pictures, if they must combine all the charms of painting, why are our *maîtres de ballet* not permitted to show on the stage of the *Opéra* three examples of their work; one founded on history, another on fable, and the last the product of their own imagination? If these masters succeeded, they would be admitted as members of the academy or received into that society. From this mark of distinction and this procedure, a spirit of emulation (precious food of the arts) would immediately be born; and dancing, encouraged by this recompense, however chimerical it might be, would, with a rapid flight, take its place beside the other arts. This academy, besides becoming more frequented, would perhaps be more distinguished; the efforts of provincial pupils would excite their comrades; dancers who had passed through it would serve as an incentive to its principal members; the tranquil life of the provinces would afford those living there the means of thinking, reflecting and writing on their art; they would forward to the society papers often instructive, the academy in its turn would be forced to reply, and this literary exchange would, by shedding new light on us, draw us little by little from our languor and obscurity. Young men who engage in dancing mechanically and without principles would undoubtedly begin again unerringly; they would learn to recognise difficulties and force themselves to surmount them, and reliable perceptors would prevent them from going astray.

It is asserted, Sir, that our academy is the abode of silence and the tomb of the talents of those who compose it. Complaints have been made that one never sees issue from it any kind of writing, either good, bad or indifferent. Reproaches have been made that it has entirely diverged from its first principles, that it meets but rarely or by chance, and never concerns itself in any way with the progress of the art which is the object of its foundation, nor with the care of instructing dancers and forming pupils. The means which I propose would inevitably silence calumny or slander, and afford the society the consideration and name which many persons refuse it, perhaps unjustly.

I shall add that its success, if it determined to take pupils, would be infinitely more assured. It would have, at least in the eyes of a multitude of masters avid of a reputation which they have not merited, the satisfaction of crediting itself with the progress of its pupils and the right of throwing the blame for their defects on those from whom they received their first lessons. "This dancer," a master will say, "was badly taught in the beginning; if he has defects it is not my fault; I have attempted the impossible. The parts in which he is distinguished belong to me, they are my work." Thus, Sir, without enlarging on the troubles of the profession, one could adroitly draw up a short reply in case of criticism and a kind of vote of confidence in case of applause. You will admit, however, that the perfection of a work depends partly on the beauty of the outline; but a pupil presented to the public is like a picture that a painter exhibits at the *Salon;* everyone admires and applauds it, or everyone blames and censures it.

Imagine then the advantage to be gained from being constantly on the watch for likely pupils taught in the provinces who would bring honour upon one by reason of the talents which one has not given them. It is only necessary to spread abroad that the pupil has been disgracefully taught, that the master has completely ruined him, that one has had an incredible labour to destroy that bad countrified manner of dancing and rectify astonishing defects. One should add that the pupil has zeal, that he responds to the pains taken with him, that he works night and day, and then bring him before a public a month afterwards.

"Let us see," people will say, "this young man dance; he is a pupil of So-and-so; he was detestable a month ago." "Yes," another will reply, "he was unbearable and as bad as he could be." The pupil enters and is applauded before he dances. However, he dances gracefully and elegantly; his attitudes are beautiful, his steps are well executed, he is brilliant *en l'air*, lively and precise *terre à terre;* what a surprise! "A miracle!" is the cry. "This master is astounding! To have made a dancer in twenty lessons! Such a thing has never been done, the talents of our century are amazing."

The master receives these praises with a modesty

which charms, while the pupil, dazzled by success and dizzy from applause, gives himself up to the deepest ingratitude. He forgets even the name of the one to whom he owes all, every sentiment of gratitude is for ever effaced from his soul. He avows, protests shamelessly that he knew nothing —as if he were in a position to judge himself; and he belauds the artfulness by which he imagines praise has been lavished upon him.

That is not all. This same pupil affords a new delight each time he appears, soon he arouses the jealousy of, and gives umbrage to, his teacher, because his style is the same, and the latter fears that his pupil will surpass him and cause him to become forgotten. What pettiness! Is it possible to persuade oneself that an able man can find no glory in making another more skilful than himself? Does it debase his merit and shatter his reputation to bring to life his talents in a pupil? Ah, Sir, would the public be ungrateful to Jélyotte if he had made a man to equal him? Would he be any the less Jélyotte? No, undoubtedly, such fears never trouble real merit, and only alarm the mediocre.

But let us return to the *Académie de Danse*. What excellent papers, what new observations, and how many instructive treatises could issue from the society, were the emulation of the members spurred and awakened by the work which would be offered to them!

It had been hoped, Sir, that the academicians and the governing body would supply the Encyclopædia with all the articles concerning the art of dancing. This object would have been better carried out by enlightened dancers rather than by M. de Cahusac.[1] The historical part belongs to the latter, but the technical part should, it seems to me, by right belong to dancers. They would have enlightened both public and dancers, and in illustrating the art would themselves become illustrious. The ingenious productions which dancing so often brings forth at Paris, and of which they could at least have given some examples, would have been perpetuated in different plates of those choregraphic charts, which, as I have said, teach nothing or very little.

[1] Louis de Cahusac (1700–1759), a French dramatic author. He composed the *libretti* for a number of Rameau's opera-ballets, but is probably best known for his history of dancing, styled *La Danse,* published 1754.

I suppose, in fact, that the academy would have engaged the collaboration in its labours of two great men, Boucher and Cochin[1] ; that an academician who understood choregraphy would have been given the task of drawing the tracks and noting the steps ; that one who was able to write the most lucidly would have explained all that which the geometrical plan could not show clearly ; that he would have taken count of the effects which each stirring picture would have produced, and of that which resulted from such and such a situation ; and finally that he would have analysed the steps and the successive *enchaînements ;* that he would have spoken of the positions of the body, the attitudes, and would have omitted nothing which could explain and make clear the miming, the pantomimic expression, and the varied sentiments of the soul by the different facial expressions.   Then Boucher, with a skilful hand, would have drawn all the groups and really interesting situations ; and M. Cochin, with a vigorous graver, would have multiplied Boucher's sketches.   You must admit, Sir, that, with the help of these two celebrated men, our academicians could easily transmit to posterity the merit of those *maîtres de ballet* and skilful dancers whose names are scarcely known to us, and who, after they have retired from the stage, have left us only a confused memory of the talents which compelled our admiration.   Choregraphy would then become interesting.   Ground plan, plan in elevation, a faithful description of these plans, everything would be presented to the eye ; the whole would explain the attitudes of the body, the expression of the heads, the contours of the arms, the position of the legs, the elegance of the dresses, the accuracy of the costumes—in fine, such a work, illustrated by the pencil and graver of two such illustrious artists, would enable one to go to the fountainhead, and I should regard it as the repository of all that art can offer of enlightenment, interest and beauty.

What a scheme, you will tell me !   What an enormous expense !   What a mighty tome !   It will be easy for me to reply to you.   First, I do not propose two mercenaries, but two artists who will treat the academy with that disinterestedness which is the sign and proof of genuine

[1] Charles Nicolas Cochin (1715-1790), a celebrated French engraver.

talent. Second, I only intend the artists for things absolutely worthy of them and their attention ; that is to say, excellent things full of fire and genius, those rare and quite novel pieces which are a source of inspiration in themselves. Thus there is economy in expense, and certainly the plates will be limited in number. More sensitive than anyone else of the glory of an academy, then of real value, why cannot I see, Sir, this project already put into execution ? And what surer means for its achievement, and for those dancers whom the academy delights to honour, to soar to immortality, than that of borrowing the wings of two artists born to engrave for ever on the temple of memory their own names and those of the persons whom they wish to commemorate ? Such an enterprise will seem their right, and I dare assert that our academicians would find in them all the resources which could be desired, when they displayed to them some models in which the capital, the centre and meeting-place of all talents, abounds, and which I have neither the boldness nor temerity to indicate to them.

There, Sir, that is what I think should be substituted for the choregraphy of our period, that art which to-day is so complicated that the eyes and intelligence lose themselves in it, because what was only the rudiments of the dance has imperceptibly become its kabbala. The perfection which it has been desired to give to the signs which correspond to steps and movements has only served to make them confusing and indecipherable. The more elaborate dancing becomes, the greater the number of signs needed, and the more unintelligible this science will be. Judge it, I pray you, by the article on choregraphy in the Encyclopædia[1] ; you will certainly look upon this art as a dancer's algebra, and I very much doubt whether the accompanying plates throw a clearer light on the obscure points of that dissertation.

I agree, you will perhaps reply, that the famous Blondy himself forbade his pupils to study this science, but at least you recognise that choregraphy is necessary to *maîtres de ballet*. No, Sir, it is an error to imagine that a capable *maître de ballet* can trace out and compose his work by his fireside. Those who labour thus will never achieve anything

[1] The *Encyclopédie* of Diderot and D'Alembert (1751-72).

but miserable combinations. You do not make dancers
move by writing in your study. The stage is the parnassus
of ingenious composers ; there, without seeking for them,
they encounter a multitude of new things ; there, everything
is connected, everything is soulful, everything is drawn in
lines of fire. One picture or situation leads naturally to
another ; figures connect together with ease and grace, the
general effect is felt at once, because a figure which is
elegant on paper ceases to be so when performed ; another
which the onlooker will find elegant in a bird's-eye view,
will not prove so to the audience in the first circle and pit.
In ballets you notice marches, counter-marches, pauses,
retreats, evolutions, groups or platoons. Now if the *maître
de ballet* have not the ability to set the great machine in
motion in the right proportion ; if he do not discover at
the first glance the inconveniences which may result from
such and such an operation ; if he have not the art to profit
by the space at his disposal ; if he do not proportion his
manœuvres to the size of his stage ; if his dispositions be
ill-conceived : if the movements which he wish to employ
be false or impossible ; if the marches be too quick, or too
slow, or ill-directed ; and time and a sense of homogeneity
be not present—in short, if the moment be ill-chosen,
nothing is perceived but confusion, fuss and tumult,
everything is in collision. It has not and cannot have
either neatness, harmony, accuracy or precision ; and
hoots and hisses are the just reward of so monstrous and
badly-executed a work. The arrangement and development
of a well-conceived grand ballet requires, Sir, knowledge,
intelligence, taste, ingenuity, a delicate tact, a wise foresight
and an all-seeing eye. And all these qualities are not
acquired by the deciphering or notation of a dance by
choregraphy ; a single moment determines the composition :
the skill consists in seizing it and turning it to account.

It is, however, sham *maîtres de ballet* who compose their
ballets, after having mutilated those of others with the help
of a note-book and certain signs which they adopt and which
provide them with a private system of choregraphy—for
the manner of drawing tracks is always the same and varies
in colouring alone. But nothing is so insipid and tedious
as a work planned on paper ; it always creates contention

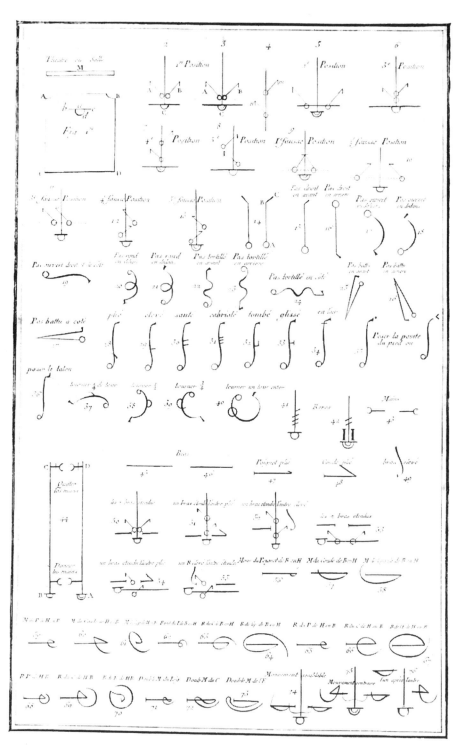

SIGNS USED IN DANCE NOTATION, XVIIITH CENTURY
From Diderot & D'Alembert's "Encyclopédie," 1751-72

and trouble. It would be amusing to see a *maître de ballet* of the *Opéra*, folio in hand, racking his brains to recollect the ballets in *Les Indes Galantes*[1] or any other opera containing dances. How many different tracks would he not have to write for a large ballet? Then add to twenty-four tracks, sometimes regular, sometimes irregular, all the complicated steps to be executed, and you will have, Sir, if you wish it, a masterpiece of writing, but loaded with so great an abundance and so confused a medley of lines, strokes, signs and characters, that your eyes would be dazzled and all the information you expected to draw from it would be, as it were, obscured by the dark web of the plan.

Moreover, do not imagine that a *maître de ballet*, after having composed the ballets of an opera to the satisfaction of the public, is necessarily obliged to preserve an exact record of these for when he revives them five or six years later. If he disdain such an aid he will only compose the ballets anew and with more taste ; he will even repair the defects which may have existed in them (for the memory of our mistakes is that which fades least) ; and if he take pencil it will not be to transfer to paper their principal forms and most striking figures ; he will certainly neglect to draw all the different paths which lead to those forms and which connect those figures ; and he will not lose time in writing the steps, nor the varied attitudes which adorn those pictures. Yes, Sir, choregraphy deadens the imagination, weakens and stifles the talents of the composer who makes use of it. He is tedious, apathetic, and incapable of invention. Instead of being the creator he was, or could be, he becomes or is nothing but a plagiarist ; he produces nothing new and his whole merit is limited to disfiguring the productions of others. Such is the effect of the numbness and species of lethargy into which this method throws the intelligence that I have seen many *maîtres de ballet* obliged to forgo the revival of their works, because they had lost their note-books and were unable to set their dancers in motion without having under their eyes the

[1] An opera-ballet in three *entrées* and a prologue, words by Fuzelier and music by Rameau, first performed on August 23rd, 1735. A year later a fourth *entrée*, entitled *Les Sauvages*, was added.

memoranda of that which others had composed. I repeat, Sir, and I maintain it, that nothing is more pernicious than a system which limits our ideas, or which does not permit us to have any, unless one is able to protect oneself from the danger in giving way to them. Enthusiasm, taste, imagination, knowledge—these are preferable to chore-graphy. These, Sir, are what inspire a profusion of novel steps, figures, pictures and attitudes. These are the inexhaustible sources of that immense variety which distinguishes the true artist from the recorder of dances.

I am, &c.

LETTER XIV

YOU desire me, Sir, to talk to you about my ballets; I accede to your request, but not without hesitation. In general, all descriptions of this kind of entertainment have two faults : they belittle the original when it is tolerable and belaud it when it is worthless.

An art gallery cannot be judged by the catalogue of the pictures it contains, neither can a work of literature be appreciated by its preface or its prospectus. So it is with ballets ; they must be seen, not once, but many times. A man of intelligence will draw up excellent plans and furnish a painter with the most noble ideas, but the merit lies in the composition and execution. If the works of Tasso, Ariosto and many other authors of similar style be opened, admirable subjects for reading can be found in them. It is easy to set such ideas on paper, and a few artistically arranged words will evoke a multitude of agreeable pictures to the imagination, but these will vanish as soon as one endeavours to put them into execution.

Nevertheless, I shall try to satisfy your curiosity in the belief that you will not judge me by the ill-drawn sketch of some ballets which the public has received with applause, which, however, has not made me forget that its indulgence far exceeds my talents.

I am very far from asserting that my productions are masterpieces ; flattering approbation has persuaded me that they have some measure of value, but I am still more convinced that they are not without faults. However it be, this slight merit and these defects belong to me alone. I have never had before my eyes those excellent models which elevate and inspire. If I had seen them, perhaps I should have been able to draw some inspiration from them. At any rate I should have studied the art of copying the work of others, and I should have forced myself to master them, or at least employ them without becoming ridiculous. This lack of instructive objects, however, excited in me a lively desire to excel, with which, perhaps, I should not have been inspired if I had possessed the facility of being only a tedious and servile imitator. Nature is the sole model I have looked upon and which I am disposed to follow, although my imagination does sometimes lead me astray. Taste, or, if you wish, a kind of instinct, warns me when I wander and recalls me to the true path. I destroy without regret all that I have created with so much labour, and my works do not interest me unless I am really moved by them. Nothing, Sir, exhausts me so much as the composition of the ballets for certain operas. The *passepieds* and *menuets* kill me, the monotony of the music enervates me, and I become as tedious as they are.

Contrariwise, expressive, harmonious and varied music, such as that to which I have composed ballets recently, suggest to me a thousand ideas, a thousand details ; it transports, exalts and inflames me, and to the different impressions it has made me experience and which have entered my soul, I owe the harmony, homogeneity, superiority, novelty, passion and that multitude of striking and singular characters which impartial judges have been able to observe in my ballets. These are the natural effects of music on dancing, and of dancing on music, when two artists are attracted to each other and when the two arts blend, unite and mutually exchange their charms to captivate and please.

It would undoubtedly be useless to talk to you of: *Les Métamorphoses Chinoises, Les Réjouissances Flamandes, La Mariée du Village, Les Fêtes du Vauxhall, Les Recrues Prussiennes, Le Bal Paré*, and a considerable number of, perhaps too many, comic ballets almost devoid of plot, being intended solely to amuse the eye, and whose whole merit lies in the novelty of the forms and in the variety and brilliancy of the figures. I do not propose either to speak to you of those which I have treated in the serious style— ballets such as I have entitled: *La Mort d'Ajax, Le Jugement de Paris, La Descente d'Orphée aux Enfers, Renaud et Armida*, etc. And I shall refrain from describing those called: *La Fontaine de Jouvence* and *Les Caprices de Galathée.*

Persuaded of your good wishes and the interest you take in all that concerns me, I think, Sir, that the description of works, which owe their existence to me entirely and which you can regard as the sole fruit of my imagination, will please you better. I shall therefore begin with that entitled: *La Toilette de Vénus, ou Les Ruses de l'Amour*, a ballet partly heroic and partly pantomimic.

The scene represents a magnificent room. Venus, clad in the most transparent garments, is at her toilet. The Games and Pleasures vie with one another in offering her everything which can add to her adornment. The Graces dress her hair, Cupid laces one of her sandals. Young Nymphs are engaged in fashioning garlands, others choose a helmet for Cupid. Still others place flowers on his costume and on the mantle which is to be his mother's chief adornment. The toilet concluded, Venus turns towards her son and appears to consult him. The little God praises her beauty and throws himself into her arms; and the first scene offers all that is most captivating in coquettish grace.

The second scene is devoted solely to the tiring of Venus, to which all the Graces attend. Some of the Nymphs are occupied in arranging the toilet table, while others carry the necessary articles to the Graces. The Games and Pleasures, no less eager to serve the Goddess, hold one a rouge box, another a patch box, others a bouquet, a necklace, and bracelets. Cupid assumes an elegant attitude, takes a mirror himself and bounds continually among the Nymphs, who, in revenge for his agility, wrest from him his bandage and quiver. He pursues them, but is stopped by three of these Nymphs, who offer him a helmet and mirror. Putting on the former, he admires himself in the latter. He runs to his mother's arms and, sighing, considers how to gain his revenge for the affront that has been put upon him. He begs Venus to aid him in his enterprise, and induces her mind to tenderness by depicting the most moving voluptuousness. Venus then displays all her graces; her movements, her attitudes, her looks conjure up the utmost pleasures of love. The Nymphs, affected beyond measure, endeavour to imitate her and assimilate all the shades she employs to captivate them. Cupid,

witnessing the impression made upon them, profits by the
moment. He deals the final blow, and in a general *entrée*
makes them experience all the passions he inspires. Their
uneasiness increases continually, they pass from tenderness
to jealousy, from jealousy to fury, from fury to despondency,
from despondency to despair ; in fine, they experience all
those varied feelings by which the heart can be moved,
but he ever recalls them to a state of happiness. The
God, satisfied and content with his victory, wishes to leave
them. He flees and they eagerly follow him, but he
escapes and disappears with his mother and the Graces.
The Nymphs run and fly after the pleasure which eludes
them.

This scene, Sir, loses everything in the perusal. You
can see neither the Goddess, nor the God, nor their
attendants. You can distinguish nothing, and in my
difficulty to explain the features, looks and movements
which the Nymphs express so well, you have only the
most imperfect and faint idea of the most lively and varied
actions.

The following scene knits up the plot. Cupid appears
alone; he revives nature with a gesture and a glance. The
scene changes, it represents a vast and sombre forest. The
Nymphs, who have never let the God out of their sight,
rush on to the stage; but how afraid they are ! They see
neither Venus nor the Graces ; the darkness of the forest,
the silence which reigns in it, fills them with fear. They
retire trembling. Cupid soon reassures them and bids
them follow him. The Nymphs consent, but he seems
to elude them by his fleetness of foot. They run after him,
but by means of many feints he always escapes. Finally,
at the moment when he appears to be in the greatest
difficulty and the Nymphs think to stop him, he disappears
in a flash, to be immediately replaced by a dozen Fauns.
This sudden and unexpected transformation produces so
grand an effect that nothing is so striking as the contrast
which results from the situation of the Nymphs and the
Fauns.

The Nymphs are the picture of innocence, the Fauns
that of ferocity. The attitudes of the latter are full of pride
and vigour ; the positions of the former express only the

fright inspired by danger. The Fauns pursue the Nymphs, who flee before them, but are soon captured. Some of the Nymphs, however, profiting by the moment of confusion into which the ardour of the pursuit has thrown the Fauns, take to flight and escape. There remain only six Nymphs for the dozen Fauns. They dispute the spoils, none of them will agree to a division, and, jealousy soon giving way to fury, they struggle and fight. The trembling and frightened Nymphs continually pass from one captor to another, as each in turn becomes victorious or vanquished. However, at the moment when the combatants appear to be occupied only with the defeat of their rivals, the Nymphs are tempted to make their escape. Six Fauns dart in pursuit, but cannot stop them, because they themselves are restrained by their pursuing adversaries. Their rage irritates them more and more. Each runs to the trees, furiously tears at the branches and rains terrible blows on his opponent. Equally skilful at guarding themselves, they throw away these objects of their futile vengeance and rage, and impetuously darting one on another they struggle with a bitterness born of madness and despair. They seize and throw one another to the ground, spring to their feet, clasp, stifle, press and strike one another. There is not a single moment of the combat which does not suggest a picture.

At last, six of the Fauns are victorious ; they trample their enemies underfoot and raise their arms for the final blow. Then six Nymphs, led by Cupid, restrain them and present them with flowers. The Nymphs, sympathising with the shame and dejection of the vanquished, let the garlands intended for the victors fall at their feet. The former remain in an attitude which depicts the most terrible sadness and prostration. Their heads are lowered, their eyes are fixed on the ground. Venus and the Graces moved by their despair, induce Cupid to be kind to them. He leaps about them, and with a light breath reanimates and brings them back to life. They are seen raising their numbed arms to invoke Venus's son, who, by his attitudes and looks, gives them, as it were, a new existence. Scarcely do they enjoy it when they perceive their enemies delighting in their good fortune and frolicking around the Nymphs.   A new resentment takes hold of them, their eyes gleam with fire.   They attack and fight them and triumph in their turn.   Ill pleased with their victory if they do not carry off the spoils, they seize them and tear off the garlands of flowers which they gloried in, but, owing to a charm cast by Cupid, these garlands divide in two.   This event again establishes peace and tranquillity among them.   The new victors and the newly-vanquished each receive the reward of victory.   The Nymphs give their hands to those who were about to die, and finally Cupid unites the Nymphs to the Fauns.

Then the symmetrical ballet commences, the mechanical beauties of the art are displayed in a *grand chaconne*, in which Cupid, Venus, the Graces, Games and Pleasures dance the principal *variations*.   At this point one might expect the action to wane, but I seized the moment when Venus, having bound Cupid with flowers, holds him in leash to prevent the God from following one of the Graces for whom he has an affection ; and during this expressive *pas* the Pleasures and Games carry the Nymphs away into the forest.   The Fauns hasten after them, and for the sake of decorum and not to present too obvious an interpretation on the remarks which Cupid addresses to his mother in regard to their disappearance, I cause these same Nymphs and Fauns to reappear an instant later.   The expression of the former, the satisfied air of the latter, depict in restrained colours during an expressive passage of the *chaconne*, pictures of voluptuousness tempered by sentiment and modesty.

This ballet, Sir, has a vigorous and continuous action. It has achieved, and I can pride myself upon it, a sensation that dancing had not hitherto produced.   This success determined me to forsake the style to which I was attached, less, I admit, from inclination, than from knowledge and habit.   From that moment I devoted myself to expressive dancing and the *danse d'action*.   I wished to depict in a larger and less elaborate manner, and I felt that I had grossly deceived myself in imagining that dancing was intended for the eyes alone, and that sight was the barrier which limited its power and extent.   For I am convinced that its power is more extensive and that it can affect the heart and the soul. I shall henceforth exert myself to make it enjoy all its advantages.

The Fauns were without *tonnelets*, and the Nymphs, Venus and the Graces were without paniers. I had proscribed masks, for they would be opposed to all expression. Mr. Garrick's method has been of great help to me. One read in the eyes and faces of my Fauns all the phases of the passions by which they were moved. A laced shoe suggesting the bark of a tree seemed to me preferable to dancing shoes. Neither the stockings nor the gloves were white. They were coloured to correspond with the flesh tints of these forest inhabitants. A simple drapery of tiger-skin covered a part of their bodies, all the rest appeared nude ; and so that the costume should not have too cold an effect and not offer too violent a contrast with the elegant dress of the Nymphs, I caused a garland of leaves mingled with flowers to be thrown over the draperies.

Again, I had thought of introducing pauses into the music, and these produced the most flattering effect. The spectator's ear suddenly ceasing to be struck by the harmony, his eye took in with more attention all the details of the pictures, the position and design of the groups, the expression of the heads and the different parts that made up the whole—nothing escaped his glance. These pauses in the music and in the movements of the body diffused a sense of calm and light ; they showed up to greater advantage the piece which followed. These are the shades which, when artistically used and tastefully arranged, afford a new and definite value to every part of the composition. But the skill consists in employing them sparingly ; they become as fatal to dancing as they sometimes are to painting if they be abused.

Let us pass to *Les Fêtes, ou Les Jalousies du Sérail.* This ballet and the one I have just described, shared the appreciation of the public ; nevertheless, they are conceived in entirely opposite styles and cannot be compared one with the other.

The stage represents a part of the harem, the foreground is occupied by a peristyle embellished with cascades and fountains. The background is formed by an arbour in the form of a circular colonnade, the intervals of which are

crowned with garlands of flowers and decorated with figures and fountains.   Farther still can be seen a waterfall of many divisions which falls into a basin.   Beyond this lies a landscape which recedes into the distance.   The women of the harem are lying on rich divans or on the ground ; they are engaged in those pursuits followed by Turkish women.

Eunuchs, both white and black, superbly dressed, enter and bring sherbert and coffee to the Sultanas ; others hasten to proffer them flowers, fruit and perfume.   One of the Sultanas, more interested in herself than in her companions, only desires a mirror ; a slave offers her one.   She admires herself with pleasure, arranges her gestures, attitudes and bearing.   Her companions, jealous of her graces, try to imitate all her movements.   This affords excuse for several *entrées*, some general, some single, which express only voluptuousness and the universal ardent desire to please their lord and master.

The charms of soft music and the murmuring of the waters are succeeded by a majestic march, danced by Mutes and the Eunuchs, both black and white, which heralds the arrival of the Sultan.

He enters hurriedly, attended by his Aga, a swarm of Janissaries, many Bostangis and four Dwarfs.   At the same moment the Eunuchs and Mutes fall on their knees, all the women bow their heads and the Dwarfs present him with baskets containing flowers and fruit.   He chooses a bouquet, and with a single gesture commands all his slaves to withdraw.

The Sultan, alone and surrounded by his wives, seems uncertain as to the choice he should make.   He walks round them with that air of indecision which a multitude of pleasing objects always inspires.   All these women endeavour to capture his heart, but it would seem that Zaïre or Zaïde must obtain the preference.   He offers the bouquet to Zaïde, and at the moment when she is about to take it a glance from Zaïre forces him to delay his decision.   He considers her, allows his gaze to wander anew, then finally returns to Zaïde, but an enchanting smile from Zaïre decides him.   He gives her the bouquet, which she accepts with rapture.   The other Sultanas express by their attitude spite and jealousy. Zaïre enjoys the confusion of her companions and defeat of her rival. The Sultan, perceiving the impression which his choice has made on the women of the harem, and wishing to increase Zaïre's triumph, commands Fatima, Zima and Zaïde to fasten on the favoured one's dress the bouquet which he has presented to her. They regretfully obey, but, despite the eagerness with which they appear to respond to the Sultan's behest, they cannot resist giving way to movements expressive of spite and despair, which they apparently stifle when they encounter their lord's eye.

The Sultan dances a voluptuous *pas de deux* with Zaïre and withdraws in her company.

Zaïde, to whom the Sultan seemed to offer the bouquet, confused and in despair, expresses in an *entrée seule* the most terrifying rage and spite. She draws a dagger and wishes to kill herself, but her companions stay her arm and hasten to turn her from this murderous design.

Zaïde is about to renounce her intention when Zaïre proudly reappears. Her presence awaken's Zaïde's jealousy in all its fury. Suddenly she darts upon Zaïre, intending to deal her the blow she had destined for herself. Zaïre adroitly evades her, seizes the dagger and raises her arm to strike Zaïde with the weapon. The women of the harem separate them ; they run first to one and then to the other. Zaïde, disarmed, takes advantage of the moment when her enemy has her arms held to throw herself on the dagger which Zaïre wears at her girdle. But the Sultanas watching over the rivals ward off the blow. At the same moment the Eunuchs, roused by the noise, enter the harem. They perceive the combat proceeding in a manner which leads them to believe that they will be unable to make peace, and they go out hurriedly to acquaint the Sultan. Meanwhile, the Sultanas part and draw away the two rivals, who make incredible efforts to free themselves, in which they are successful. Hardly are they free than they dart furiously on each other. The frightened women fly between them to stop their blows. At this moment the Sultan enters : the change consequent on his arrival produces a striking theatrical effect. Pleasure and tenderness at once succeed grief and rage. Zaïre, so far from complaining, displays a generosity common to those possessed of fine feelings. Her serenity reassures the Sultan and soothes his fear that he had lost the object of his affections. This calm brings joy to the harem, and the Sultan permits the Eunuchs to hold a festival in Zaïre's honour. The dance becomes general.

Zaïre and Zaïde are reconciled in a *pas de deux*. The Sultan dances with them a *pas de trois*, in which he always displays a preference for Zaïre.

This festival ends with a well-executed *contredanse*. The last figure presents a group disposed on a high throne approached by steps. The group is composed of the women of the harem, and the Sultan with Zaïre and Zaïde seated on either side. It is crowned by a large canopy, whose curtains are supported by slaves. On each side of the stage there is a group composed of Bostangis, white Eunuchs, black Eunuchs, Mutes, Janissaries, and Dwarfs prostrate at the foot of the Sultan's throne.

That, Sir, is a very feeble description of a series of scenes which really interest everyone. The moment when the Sultan makes his choice and leads away his favourite, the fight between the women, the group they form on the Sultan's arrival, that sudden change, that clash of feelings, that love which all women evince for each other and which they all express in different ways, are contrasted in a manner which I cannot convey to you. I am likewise powerless in regard to the simultaneous scenes which I placed in this ballet. The pantomime is but a sketch, the pictures which result from it are as quick as lightning, they only last for an instant and as quickly give place to others. Now, Sir, in a well-conceived ballet, only a little dialogue and few pauses are needed, the heart must be continually moved. Hence, how can the lively expression of emotion and the animated action of pantomime be described ? It is for the soul to paint, and the soul to understand the picture.

The themes of the ballets of which I have spoken take far less time to execute than to read. Outward signs which reveal a sentiment become cold and lifeless, if they be not quickly followed by other signs indicative of the new passions which succeed them. Again, it is necessary to divide the action among several characters. Several persons making the same efforts and movements with a constantly increasing agitation would weary player and spectator alike. It is important, then, to avoid prolixity, if one wish to allow expression its true force, gestures their true energy, features their true manner, eyes their true eloquence, attitudes and positions their true grace.

Critics accustomed to reading novels will perhaps assert that the ballet, *Les Fêtes, ou Les Jalousies du Sérail*, errs against the dress and customs of the Levantines. They will conceive it ridiculous to introduce Janissaries and Bostangis into that part of the harem sacred to the Sultan's wives, and they will object further that there are no dwarfs in Constantinople and that the Sultan does not like them. I shall agree with the justice of their remarks and the extent of their knowledge, but I shall reply that if my ideas have falsified truth, they have never offended verisimilitude, and then I may have recourse to the necessary liberties which all authors are allowed to employ in much more important works than ballets.

If one were too scrupulous in depicting the characters, manners and customs of certain nations, the pictures would often be poor and monotonous in composition. Again, would it not be unjust to condemn a painter for the ingenious liberties he had taken, if these same liberties contributed to the perfection, variety and elegance of his pictures ?

When the characters are sustained so that those of the nation represented are never changed and nature is not concealed under embellishments which are foreign to and degrade it; when the expression of sentiment is faithful so that the colouring is true, the shading artistically contrived, the positions noble, the groups and masses ingenious and beautiful, and the design correct; then the picture is excellent and achieves its effect.

I think, Sir, that neither a Turkish nor a Chinese festival would appeal to our countrymen, if we had not the art to embellish it, and I am persuaded that the style of dancing common to those people would never be captivating. This kind of exactitude in costume and imitation will only present a very insipid spectacle, unworthy of a public which only applauds in proportion as artists possess the art of bringing delicacy and taste to the different productions which they offer to it.

If those who have criticised me for the supposed liberty which I had taken in introducing Bostangis and Janissaries into the harem had been witnesses of the execution, distribution and progress of my ballet, they would have seen that these persons who have offended them at a hundred leagues' distance never enter into that part of the harem set apart for the women. They only appear in the garden, and I employed them in that scene simply as part of a procession to render the Sultan's arrival more imposing and majestic.

Besides, Sir, a criticism based on a programme alone falls to the ground, because it is founded on nothing. A painter's merit is judged by his pictures; similarly, a *maître de ballet* must be judged by the effect of his groups, situations, theatrical effects, ingenious figures, striking forms and the homogeneity which pervades his work. To judge our efforts without seeing them is equivalent to criticising an object in the dark.

I am, &c.

TWO more ballets, Sir, and my object will be fulfilled, because it is time I brought my remarks to an end. I have said sufficient to persuade you of all the difficulties of an art which is easy only for those who skim the surface, and who imagine that the action of rising from the ground an inch higher than others, or the idea of some *moulinets* or *ronds*, will attract to them every approbation. No matter the style, the farther one goes the more the obstacles increase, and the more distant appears the object it is desired to attain. Again, Sir, the most strenuous labour affords the greatest artists but a disquieting gleam which only reveals their inadequacy, while the self-satisfied ignoramus surrounded by the deepest gloom flatters himself that he has nothing more to learn.

The ballet which I wish to describe to you is entitled: *L'Amour Corsaire, ou l'Embarquement pour Cythère.* The scene takes place on the seashore of the Isle of Misogyny. Unfamiliar trees embellish this land. From one side of the stage is perceived an antique altar erected to the divinity worshipped by the inhabitants. A statue representing a man plunging a knife into a woman's breast is erected above the altar. The inhabitants of this island are cruel and barbarous ; it is their custom to sacrifice to their god all the women whom misfortune casts up on their coasts. They impose their law on all the men who escape the fury of the waves.

The first scene opens with the entrance of a stranger saved from a shipwreck. He is conducted to the altar by which stand two High Priests. Some of the islanders are disposed round the altar, holding in their hands clubs used for exercise, while others celebrate in a mysterious dance the arrival of this new proselyte. He sees himself forced to promise solemnly to slay with the knife with which he is armed, the first woman whom a too cruel destiny brings to that island. Hardly has he begun to pronounce the terrible oath at which he himself shudders, although deep in his heart he makes a vow to disobey the new god whose worship he embraces, than the ceremony is interrupted by shrieks uttered at the sight of a long-boat tossed by a terrible storm, and by a lively dance which announces the wild joy born of the hope of seizing some new victim. In the boat can be seen a woman and a man who raise their hands to heaven and cry for help. As the boat approaches, Dorval (such is the stranger's name) believes he recognises his sister and her friend. He looks attentively, his heart divided between pleasure and fear. At last he sees that they are out of danger and gives way to inexpressible delight, but this joy is soon counterbalanced by the thought of the terrible place he inhabits, and this fatal reflection plunges him into the most profound dejection and grief.

The eagerness which he displayed at first has deceived the Misogynians. They thought they saw in him an inviolable zeal and an unbreakable attachment to their laws. Meanwhile, Clairville and Constance (so the two are called) land at last. Death is shown in their features, their eyes are almost closed, bristling hair reveals their terror. A pale and livid tint depicts the horror of the fate which has pursued them a thousand times and which they still dread, but what is their surprise when they feel themselves embraced. They recognise Dorval and throw themselves into his arms, they can scarcely believe their eyes. All three can hardly tear themselves apart, their delight is expressed by all the outward signs of the purest joy. They shed copious tears which are the undoubted signs of the different feelings by which they are swayed. At this moment the situation changes. A savage presents Dorval with the knife with which he must stab Constance to the heart, and commands him to plunge it into her breast.

Dorval, indignant at so barbarous a command, seizes the knife and would strike the Misogynian, but Constance, freeing herself from her lover's arms, stays the blow which her brother was about to deal. The savage seizes the weapon, disarms Dorval, and is about to pierce the breast of the woman who has just saved his life. Clairville arrests the traitor's arm and snatches the weapon from him. Dorval and Clairville, equally revolted at the brutal inhumanity of this island's inhabitants, stand beside Constance. They clasp her tightly in their arms; their bodies form a rampart against the ferocity of their enemies, and their eyes flashing with anger seem to defy the Misogynians.

The latter, furious at this resistance, command the savages armed with clubs to tear the victim from the arms of the two strangers and drag her to the altar. Dorval and Clairville, stimulated by the danger, wrest the weapons from the hands of two of these cruel men. They rush into the fight with bold ardour, returning every moment to rally round Constance. They do not lose sight of her for a moment; while she, trembling and distraught, and fearing to lose two persons so dear to her, gives way to despair. The Priests, aided by several savages, fling themselves upon her and drag her to the altar. At this moment, summoning up all her courage, she struggles with them, and, seizing the knife from one of the attendants, stabs him with it. Freed for a moment, she flings herself into her lover's arms, but is soon torn from him. Escaping once more, she returns to him. At last, overcome by numbers, Dorval and Clairville, almost succumbing to their wounds, are bound with chains. Constance is dragged to the foot of the altar, the symbol of barbarism. The Priest's arm is raised, the blow is about to fall, when the God of Lovers stays the uplifted arm and lays a charm on the island which renders every inhabitant motionless. This sudden change from excited movement to immobility produces an astonishing effect. Constance inanimate at the feet of the High Priest, Dorval and Clairville almost blinded, fall back into the arms of the savages.

The weather changes for the better, the waves subside, calm follows the storm. Tritons and Naiads gambol in the sea, and a well-appointed ship appears in the offing.

It reaches land. Cupid drops the anchor and disembarks, followed by the Nymphs, Games and Pleasures; while waiting the God's command, this gay company forms in battle array. The Misogynians recover from the ecstasy and immobility into which Cupid had plunged them. One of his glances recalls Constance to life. Dorval and Clairville, never doubting that their liberator must be a god, prostrate themselves at his feet. The savages, enraged at seeing their religion profaned, all raise their clubs to massacre the worshippers and followers of the son of Venus ; they even turn their rage and fury against him, but how can mortals prevail when Cupid decrees ? A single glance from him stays every weapon of the Misogynians. He commands their altar to be overturned, their infamous divinity to be destroyed ; the Games and Pleasures obey his behests, the altar totters under their blows, the statue collapses and is broken into pieces. A new altar appears and takes the place of that just destroyed. It is of white marble. Garlands of roses, jessamine and myrtle add to its elegance, columns spring out of the ground to adorn this altar, and a rich canopy borne by a group of *amorini* descends from the skies. The ends of the canopy are supported by Zephyrs, who direct it so that it rests on the four columns surrounding the altar. The ancient trees on the island give place to myrtles, orange trees and groves of roses and jessamine.

The Misogynians become furious at the sight of their divinity cast down and their religion profaned, but Cupid only permits their anger to break forth at intervals. He always stops them when they are about to strike. The moments when this spell renders them motionless afford a multitude of pictures and groups which differ completely in their positions and arrangement, but which all express the most terrible fury. The pictures made by the Nymphs are entirely opposed to them in style and colour. Against the blows with which the Misogynians threaten them, they offer only airs and graces, tender and voluptuous looks. However, Cupid commands them to fight and vanquish the savages, who offer only a feeble resistance. If they have the strength to raise an arm to deliver a blow, they lack the courage to carry out their design. Finally, the clubs fall from their hands. Defeated and defenceless, they throw themselves at the knees of their victors, who, tender by nature, pardon them and bind them with garlands of flowers. Cupid, gratified, unites Clairville to Constance, the Misogynians to the Nymphs, and bestows on Dorval a young Nymph called Zenéide whom he has carefully trained.

This ballet opens with a triumphal march; the Nymphs lead the vanquished in leash, Cupid arranges the festival and general rejoicing commences. Cupid, Clairville and Constance, Dorval and Zenéide, the Games and the Pleasures, perform the principal dances. The executants of the stately *contredanse* in this ballet break up gradually into couples, and one after the other pass on board the vessel. Little benches arranged in different ways and of different heights serve, so to speak, as a pedestal to this amorous band, and present a large group elegantly arranged. The anchor is raised, the Zephyrs blow out the sails, the vessel gets under weigh, and, impelled by favourable breezes, voyages to Cythera.

I shall now pass to the Spanish ballet called *Jaloux sans Rival*, and I forewarn you that there are again fights with daggers. A misanthrope is known as the man with the green ribbons, perhaps I shall be called the man with the daggers. When the art of pantomime be considered, when the narrow limitations prescribed for it be examined, when, finally, the insufficiencies of what is called quiet dialogue be weighed, and when it is recalled to what degree it is subordinate to the rules of painting, which, like pantomime, can express moments only, I cannot be censured for choosing all those which by their combination and sequence can stir the heart and move the soul. I do not know if I have done well to devote myself to this style of work, but the tears which many scenes in my ballets have made the public shed, the lively emotion which they have caused, persuade me that if I have not yet attained my aim, I have nevertheless found the road which leads to it. I do not flatter myself in the least that I am able to bridge the immense distance which separates me from it, this success is only attainable by those to whom genius lends wings; but at least I shall have the satisfaction of having been a pioneer. To point out the way which leads to perfection is an advantage which satisfies him who has not the strength to reach it.

Fernando is Inez's lover; Clitandre, a French dandy,

is the lover of Beatrix, the friend of Inez. These are the characters about which the plot revolves ; Clitandre, in the course of a game of chess, violently quarrels with Beatrix.

Inez seeks to reconcile Clitandre and Beatrix. The latter, proud by nature, withdraws. Clitandre follows her in desperation. He returns a moment later and begs Inez to help him. She promises to intercede in his favour, but explains to him the danger she runs in being seen alone with him, as she fears the jealousy of Fernando. The Frenchman, always vivacious and more occupied with his love affairs than with Inez's anxieties, falls on his knees to exhort her not to forget to speak to Beatrix. Fernando appears, and without asking any explanation furiously attacks Clitandre. He seizes Clitandre's hand as he is about to kiss that of Inez, who in her turn makes efforts to defend herself. At the same moment he draws a dagger to strike Clitandre, but Inez parries the blow, and Beatrix, attracted by the noise, places herself in front of her lover. At this instant, the Spaniard interprets Inez's sentiments to her disadvantage, he mistakes her compassion for tenderness, her fears for love ; excited by the passions which jealousy awakens in his heart, he frees himself from Inez and leaps on Clitandre. The latter takes to his heels and escapes the danger, but the Spaniard, in despair at not having been able to vent his rage, promptly returns towards Inez to bestow on her the blow intended for his imagined rival.

He wishes to strike her, but the movement that she makes to flee the threatening arm stays his jealousy, and the dagger falls from his grasp. A gesture of Inez seems to reproach her lover with his injustice. Despairing of surviving a suspicion of infidelity, she falls into an armchair. Fernando, still jealous, but ashamed of his violence, throws himself on to another seat. The two lovers display a picture of despair and wrath. Their eyes seeking and avoiding each other by turns exhibit a picture of anger and pity. Inez draws a letter from her bosom, Fernando follows suit ; each one reads the most tender sentiments, but both, feeling themselves deceived, spitefully tear up these first tokens of their love. Both annoyed at these signs of contempt, they look attentively at each other's portrait, and, seeing nothing but signs of infidelity and treachery, they cast them at their feet. Fernando, however, expresses by his gestures and looks how much this sacrifice has wounded his heart; by a violent effort he has got rid of a portrait so dear to him. Sorrowfully he has let it fall, or rather allowed it to slip through his hands. At this moment he sinks into his chair and gives way to sadness and despair.

Beatrix, witnessing this scene, endeavours to reconcile the lovers and bring them together again. Inez makes the first advances, but, perceiving that Fernando does not respond at all to her entreaties, she takes flight. Beatrix stops her at once, and the Spaniard, seeing that his mistress wishes to avoid him, flees in his turn, appearing as if overwhelmed by vexation.

Beatrix perseveres and continues to urge them to make peace. To effect this she makes them take hands; both require pressing, but she succeeds at last in bringing them together and reuniting them. Then she regards them with a mischievous smile. The two lovers, not daring to look at each other, despite their anxiety to do so, stand back to back; by slow degrees they turn round. Inez in a glance assures Fernando's pardon. He joyfully kisses her hand; and all three retire full of unbounded joy.

As they depart, Clitandre appears on the scene. He enters alone, his features suffused with fear and anxiety. He seeks his mistress, but, perceiving Fernando, quickly takes to flight. The latter wishes to prove his gratitude to Beatrix, but, since nothing resembles love so much as friendship, Inez, who surprises him in the act of kissing Beatrix's hand, takes the opportunity to revenge herself for the scene of jealousy which her lover made her suffer, and in her turn feigns to be jealous. The Spaniard, believing her to be really affected by this passion, seeks to undeceive her by affording her new proofs of his tenderness. She appears unmoved by them, and, glancing at him with flashing eyes, shows him a dagger. He shudders, recoils with fright, and rushes forward to tear it from her, but she pretends to strike herself with it; she reels and falls into the arms of her attendants. Seeing this, Fernando stays motionless, and, thinking only of his despair, gives himself up to it entirely, and is tempted to take his own life. All the Spaniards fling themselves upon him and disarm him. Enraged, he struggles with them and seeks to resist their efforts. He fells many of them, but, overcome by weight of numbers and his own grief, his strength diminishes gradually, his limbs give way under him, his eyes grow dim and close, his features betray the approach of death, and he falls unconscious into the arms of the Spaniards.

Inez, who at the commencement of this scene enjoyed the pleasure of a vengeance which she believed innocent, and the sequel to which she did not foresee, perceiving its sad effects, gives the most convincing tokens of the sincerity of her repentance. She flies to her lover, folds him tenderly in her arms, takes him by the hand, and strives to recall him to life. Fernando opens his eyes, his gaze is troubled, he turns his head towards Inez, but what is his astonishment ! He can hardly believe his eyes. He cannot persuade himself that Inez still lives, and, doubting his good fortune, expresses in turn his surprise, fear, joy, tenderness and delight. He falls at the knees of his mistress, who receives him in her arms with transports of the most passionate love.

The different events produced by this scene makes the action general ; every heart is filled with a pleasure which Fernando, Inez, Beatrix and Clitandre express in their dances. After some *pas seuls* which depict joy and delight, the ballet is concluded with a general *contredanse*.

It is easy to perceive, Sir, that this ballet is simply a combination of the most striking scenes in our dramatic literature. They are pictures by the best masters which I have brought together.

The first is taken from the work of Diderot, the second is a theatrical effect conceived by myself—I refer to the moment when Fernando raises his hand against Clitandre. The next is taken from a scene of *Mahomet*, in which the hero is about to stab Irene, who tells him as she flees before the blow :

> *Ton bras est suspendu ! qui t'arrête ? ose tout ;*
> *Dans un cœur tout à toi laisse tomber le coup.*[1]

[1] Your arm is uplifted, who stays you? dare all ;
Plunge your weapon in a heart devoted to you.

The scene of spitefulness, the torn-up letters and contemptuous casting away of the portraits, is borrowed from Molière's *Le Dépit Amoureux*. The reconciliation of Fernando and Inez is simply that of Mariane and Valère adroitly brought about by Dorine in *Tartuffe*. Inez's pretended jealousy is an invention. Fernando's wildness, his rage, fury, despair, and prostration, are imitated from the scenes of rage in Racine's *Oreste*. The final reconciliation is copied from Crebillon's *Rhadamiste* and *Zénobie*. My work consisted in simply linking together these pictures.

You observe, Sir, that this ballet is simply an attempt made by me to ascertain the public taste and convince myself of the possibility of being able to express tragedy in terms of dancing. This ballet was a complete success, not even excepting the scene of spitefulness acted partly sitting and partly standing; it was as lively, as animated, and as realistic as the others. This entertainment has already lasted for ten months, and still affords pleasure ; the sure effect of dancing with action, it always appears new because it speaks to the soul and interests alike the heart and the eye.

I have lightly passed over matters of detail to spare you any tedium they might occasion you, and I shall conclude by some reflections on the obstinacy, negligence and idleness of dancers and on the ease with which the public yields to customary applause.

If, Sir, one were to ask all those who applaud indifferently, and who would think they had wasted the price of admission if they had not stamped their feet or clapped their hands, for their opinion of dancing and ballets, what would be their answers ? " Marvellous," they would reply, " they are wonderfully good, these arts are both agreeable and astonishing." Point out to them that alterations are necessary, that the dancing is indifferent, that the ballets have but the single merit of design, that expressiveness has been neglected, that pantomime is unknown, that the themes are senseless, that the subjects intended to be expressed are too trivial or too vast, and that there should be a considerable reform in the theatre, and you will be regarded as a fool and a maniac. They cannot credit that dancing and ballets can procure them any greater pleasure. " Let dancers continue," they will add, " to execute beautiful *pirouettes* and *entrechats*, to remain a long time on tip-toe, to show us the difficulties of the art, to shake their legs with the same quickness, and we shall rest content. We do not desire any change, everything is excellent and nothing can be more pleasing." But dancing, persons of taste will continue, only affords you mediocre sensations, whereas you would experience much keener ones if this art were carried to that degree of perfection it can attain. "We do not wish," they will reply, " dancing and ballets to affect us and make us shed tears ; we do not wish to regard this art seriously ; logic would detract from its charm ; folly, rather than reason, should direct its movements. Intelligence would destroy it ; we mean to laugh during ballets, chat during tragedy, and talk about little suppers and carriages during comedy."

There, Sir, that is the general condition of affairs. Is it possible that creative genius will always be persecuted ? To be a lover of truth is a title which disgusts all those who fear it. M. de Cahusac reveals the beauty of our art, he suggests necessary adornments ; he does not desire to take anything away from dancing ; on the contrary, he only seeks to point out a sure path in which dancers cannot go astray ; they disdain to follow it. Diderot,[1] the philosopher and friend of nature, that is to say, of simple truth and beauty, seeks likewise to enrich the French stage with subjects drawn more from humanity than his own imagination. He would like to substitute pantomime for affectation, a natural voice for the stilted diction of art, simple dress for gew-gaws and tinsel, truth for fable, wit and common sense for involved dialogue and for all ill-painted portraits which caricature and distort nature. He would like French comedy to deserve the glorious title of a school of manners, that contrasts were less startling and more artistic, that virtue should not need to be opposed to vice in order to be pleasing and seductive, because over-emphasised shadows, far from giving relief and value to

[1] Denis Diderot (1713-1784), an eminent French philosopher, savant, and author.

objects, weaken and obscure them. But all his efforts have been in vain.[1]

M. de Cahusac's treatise on dancing is as necessary to dancers as the study of chronology is indispensable to those who wish to write history. However, he has been criticised by dancers, he has even aroused the insipid pleasantries of those who for certain reasons can neither read nor understand him. How the word *pantomime* has offended those who dance in the serious style. " It would be a fine thing," they say, " to see this kind of part danced in pantomime ! " You must admit, Sir, that one must be entirely ignorant of the significance of the word to use it thus. I would much rather it were said to me : " I renounce intelligence, I wish to have nothing to do with the soul, I wish to be a brute all my life."

Many dancers who exclaim about the impossibility of uniting pantomime to mechanical execution, and who have made neither endeavour nor any effort to succeed in it, yet attack M. de Cahusac's work with very feeble weapons. They reproach him for not knowing the technique of the art, and thence conclude that his arguments are not based on sound principles. What nonsense ! Is it necessary to know how to execute a *gargouillade* and *entrechat* in order to judge dancing properly, to point out what is lacking and to indicate what is needed ? Must one be a dancer to perceive what little wit prevails in a *pas de deux*, the nonsense usually to be encountered in ballets, the lack of expression of the executants and the mediocrity of the talents of the composers ? What would be said of a playwright who would not submit to the judgment of the pit because all the spectators had not the talent to compose verses ?

If M. de Cahusac had confined himself to dance steps, to formal movements of the arms, to *enchaînements* and complicated combinations of *temps*, he would have run the risk of going astray ; but he has abandoned all these clumsy details to those who have only arms and legs. It is not for them that he has meant to write, he has treated solely of the poetry of the arts; he has dealt with its essence and character ; woe to all those who can neither enjoy nor

[1] A reference to Diderot's *Paradoxe sur le Comédien*, in which he expounds his theories regarding the art of acting.

understand him. Let us speak the truth, the style which he proposes is difficult, but is it any the less beautiful? It is the only one suited to dancing and able to embellish it.

Great actors will be of Diderot's opinion, it is only the mediocre ones who will exclaim against the style he indicates. Why? Because what is taken from life must be expressed by men and not by automata; it demands proportions which cannot be acquired if one do not carry the seed in oneself, and it is not only a question of imitation but of feeling keenly and having a soul.

One day I said to an actor: "We must act *Le Père de Famille* and *Le Fils Naturel*[1]." "They would have no effect on the stage," he replied. "Have you read those two dramas?" "Yes," he answered. "Well, were you not touched? Was your soul quite unaffected, your heart unmoved, and did your eyes refuse to shed tears at such simple but touching pictures which the author has painted so naturally?" "I have experienced," he said, "all these emotions." "Why, then," I replied, "do you doubt the effect which these pieces would produce on the stage since they have captivated you, although deprived of the charms of illusion which the stage would afford them and of the new strength they would acquire from being played by good actors?" "Therein lies the difficulty; it would be hard," he continued, "to find many capable of acting these pieces; these simultaneous scenes would be awkward to render well; the pantomimic action would be the rock on which the majority of actors would founder. A mimed scene is the real difficulty, it is the touchstone of the true actor. Those unfinished sentences, those sighs, those hardly uttered sounds, demand a truthfulness, soul, expression and intelligence which few possess; that simplicity of dress, depriving the actor of the embellishment of art, allows him to be seen as he is. His height not being increased by the elegance of his headdress, he would need to please by his natural gifts. Nothing would conceal his imperfections, and the eyes of the spectator, being no longer dazzled by tinsel and gew-gaws, would be fixed solely on the actor." "I agree," I replied, "that simplicity in any style demands the greatest perfection; that beauty can be simple and

[1] Dramas by Denis Diderot.

becoming, and that the less she is clothed the more graceful she is." But it is neither the fault of Diderot nor that of M. de Cahusac if great talents be rare, they both demand a perfection which can be only attained by emulation, the style they have treated of is the only true style, it borrows its features and graces from nature alone.

If the advice and counsels of Diderot and M. de Cahusac be never followed, if the paths they indicate to arrive at perfection be disdained, how can I expect to succeed ? No, undoubtedly, Sir, and it would be rash to think so.

I know that the frivolous fear of innovation always stays unambitious actors ; none the less, I do not ignore that custom makes mediocre talents cling to the traditions of their profession. I conceive that imitation of all kinds has charms which captivate all those without taste and intelligence. The reason is simple, it is less difficult to copy than to create.

How many talents go astray through servile imitation ! How many good dispositions are stifled and actors ignored through having quitted the style and manner suitable to them, and having been forced to take up what is opposed to their nature ! How many bad actors and detestable caricaturists have forsaken their natural path, renounced their true characters, their voices, walk, gestures and appearance to borrow the acting, pronunciations, bearing, expression and features which disfigure them so that they offer only a ridiculous caricature of the originals they have wished to copy. How many dancers, painters and musicians have ruined themselves by following that easy but pernicious road, which would lead imperceptibly to the destruction and annihilation of the arts, did not the ages always produce some rare men who, taking nature as their model and genius as their guide, raise themselves to perfection with one bold flight by virtue of their own wings !

All those persons who are dominated by imitation will invariably forget beautiful nature in order to think only of a model which attracts and captivates them, a model generally imperfect in itself and of which the copy can never please.

Question the dancers ; enquire why they never take the trouble to be original and afford their art a simpler form, a truer expression and a more natural appearance. They will tell you, in order to excuse their indolence and sloth, that they are afraid of exciting ridicule, that it is dangerous to innovate and create, that the public is accustomed to such and such a style, and that to diverge from it would displease them. Such are the reasons on which they rely to restrain the arts from caprice and change, because they ignore the fact that they are children of nature and ought to follow her alone and never stray from the laws she prescribes. Finally, they will exert themselves to persuade you that it is more glorious to vegetate and languish in the shadow of originality which ever eclipses and overwhelms them, than to take the pains to be original themselves.

Diderot has had no other aim than that of perfecting our stage; he wished to bring back to nature all the actors who had strayed from her. M. de Cahusac likewise recalled dancers to truth. But everything they have said has appeared false, because it has been presented in the simplest manner. No one has been willing to admit that it only required intelligence to put their precepts into practice. Can one deny the lack of it? Is it possible to confess that one has no expression? This would imply that one had no soul. One may say : " I have no lungs." But I have never heard a person say : " I have no feelings." Dancers sometimes admit that they have no strength, but they do not display the same frankness when it is a question of speaking of the sterility of their imagination. Finally, *maîtres de ballet* naïvely declare that they do not compose quickly, and that their profession wearies them. But they must admit that they in turn weary the spectator, that they are cold, prolix, monotonous and uninspired. Such, Sir, are the majority of men who are members of the theatrical profession. They all consider themselves faultless. Is it not astonishing that those who have exerted themselves to undeceive them, should be disgusted and even regret having attempted to disabuse them?

Self-esteem in all conditions and in all states is an inexcusable malady. It is useless to seek to bring art back to nature, everyone deserts her. No power can force dancers to return to her standard and rally under the ensigns of truth and simplicity. Such a change would be too laborious and too hard for them. Hence it was easier to say that M. de Cahusac spoke as a writer and not as a dancer, and that the manner he proposed was extravagant. For the same reason they exclaimed that *Le Fils Naturel* and *Le Père de Famille* were not suitable for the stage, and it has been easier to express an opinion than attempt to act them, so that the actors are right and the playwrights fools. Their works are only the dreams of tedious moralists and the products of ill humour, they have neither value nor merit. How could they have any ? For you do not find in them all the fashionable sayings, all the caricatures, little epigrams and jokes. In Paris, it is the infinitely petty that pleases. Once upon a time it was the custom to speak of little children, little actors, little violinists, little Englishmen and little horses at the fairs.

It would be advantageous, Sir, for the greater part of those who devote themselves to dancing and ballets to have masters who would teach them everything intimately connected with their profession which they ought to learn. The majority of them disdain and sacrifice all the knowledge it is important for them to have to a despicable idleness, and a manner of living and dissipation which degrades the art and debases the artist. This evil mode of life, with which they are only too justly reproached, is the source of the fatal prejudice which reigns universally among the persons who enter the theatrical profession, a prejudice which would soon disappear, despite the bitter censure of the very illustrious cynic of this age, if they sought to distinguish themselves by their daily life and the superiority of their talents.

THE END